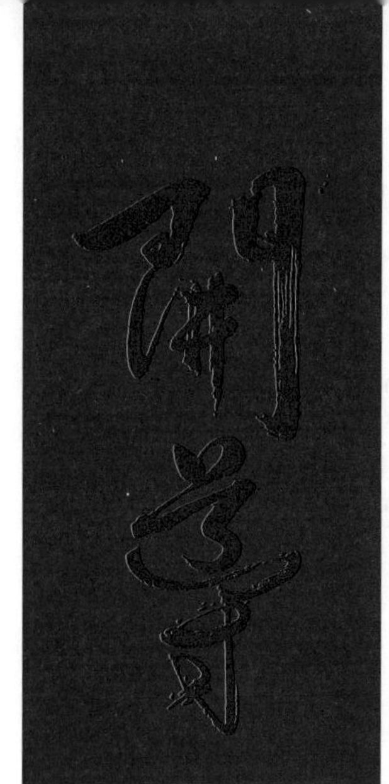

Guiding Your School Community to Live a Culture of Caring and Learning

The Process Is Called Tribes

Jeanne Gibbs

Published in the United States of America by

CENTERSOURCE SYSTEMS, LLC
7975 Cameron Drive, Suite 500, Windsor, California 95492

Library of Congress Cataloging-in-Publication Data
Gibbs, Jeanne
Guiding your school community to live a culture of caring and learning : the process is called Tribes / by Jeanne Gibbs.
p. cm.
Includes bibliographical references.
ISBN 978-0-932762-12-2 (pbk.)
1. Group work in education—United States. 2. Classroom environment—United States. 3. Academic achievement—United States. I. Title.

LB1032.G527 2007
371.2'01—dc22

2007007249

Illustrations: Pat Ronzone, Sausalito, CA
Book Design: Lynn Bell, Monroe Street Studios, Santa Rosa, CA
Printing: Creel Printing, LLC, Las Vegas, NV

PRINTED IN THE UNITED STATES OF AMERICA
10 9 8 7 6 5 4 3 2 1

ACKNOWLEDGEMENTS

The material in this book is reflective of the combined efforts of many people representing many areas of administration. We are very grateful to Judi Fenton, Nancy Latham, and Aileen Hokama who devoted so much time to telling their stories. We are also grateful to the many calls from administrators who express the way the process works within their schools. Thanks go to Annette Griffith who has shared many creative ideas, and to the countless others known and unknown who have contributed over the years to this process.

We extend our sincere thanks to Lynn Bell for her outstanding book design, text layout and computer graphics. We also especially appreciate Pat Ronzone, our wonderful illustrator, for making the book a delight to read.

—Jeanne Gibbs

◇

CONTENTS

CHAPTER 1 Opening the Gate 1

CHAPTER 2 A People Growing Culture 17

CHAPTER 3 The Roots of Leadership—Building Community and Collegiality 29

CHAPTER 4 Initiating the Journey 43

CHAPTER 5 Creating the Culture 55

CHAPTER 6 Sustaining and Extending the Culture 77

APPENDIX A Professional Development for Teachers Leads the Way 97

APPENDIX B A Fact Sheet on Tribes TLC® 105

APPENDIX C A Model and Promising Program 107

APPENDIX D Evaluation of Tribes Learning Communities 111

APPENDIX E What Is It About Tribes? 115

Notes 117

About the Author 122

CHAPTER 1

Opening the Gate—An Invitation

If you are one of those dedicated school leaders who has been trying to transform your school or district into an exciting community of learners, come on along. Perhaps you have had teachers trained to use the Tribes Learning Communities process and wonder how to use it throughout your school. You want to have the faculty, support staff, parents, bus drivers, custodians, cafeteria and resource people relate to students in a challenging and supportive way. You want everyone to take responsibility for maintaining a caring culture and succeed in their own roles as never before. One way or another you have learned that the process called Tribes TLC® (Tribes Learning Communities) not only can transform classroom teaching and learning but also management and support for the school system.[1] No doubt about it—that would make your job a lot easier!

Each new journey needs a symbol to inspire and carry hope for the explorers along the way. For this journey we would like you to carry the expressive Chinese symbol, an image of guidance. Guidance is not the way of traditional management but is a sound and caring leadership that will call forth the personal best in everyone. It is the best way, perhaps the only way, to create a high performing school over time.

This book will illuminate a way for you to discover the "wellspring of possibilities" referred to in the meaning of this Chinese symbol.

...An open gate
with two brilliant lanterns pointing to the source,
the well-spring of all possibilities,
leading the way to the spring,
step by step,
with wisdom and care.[2]

SPECIFIC GOALS OF THIS BOOK

As many of you know, this small book has taken several years to hatch. The only way that this author has ever worked on material pertaining to the process of Tribes has been to hang out, observe and question the experts using Tribes. Teachers, principals, program specialists, parents and kids have all been consultants. This is the reason Tribes has survived so many years. It keeps growing as all of you let us know what works and what does not work. The most amazing thing is that nine times out of ten, feedback from you, our experts, is confirmed by educational and organizational studies.

The administrators and school leaders who helped to plan this book were clear that it should define the *why, what* and *how* of using the community building process of Tribes at a management and leadership level. The first chapters are the *why* and *what* needs to happen, and the last chapters are *how to* do it. It may be tempting just to skip to the *how-to-do-it* section right away. But that's a "no no." It would be like a teacher just skipping over what Tribes is all about and jumping into using strategies and energizers without knowing the integral process. By reading "step-by step," you will…

learn why and how the positive Tribes culture, if carefully facilitated, will develop community throughout an entire educational system

gain an additional framework for participatory planning (teacher collegiality and community responsibility), and

understand how to initiate, support and sustain the Tribes process over a long period of time in your school community.

A CHANGING ROLE

True to the process of Tribes, first we need to develop inclusion with you by trying to meet you where you are. We're guessing that you are one of those hard working idealists committed to improving the teaching-learning outcomes for students and staff. Your busy days may include:

- communicating with district administration
- communicating with staff, parents and community agencies
- administering student discipline, attendance and safety policies
- administering personnel practices and contracts
- administering resources/time, money, people, facilities
- facilitating collaborative decision-making
- administering curriculum and instructional policies
- planning for professional development, and/or
- maintaining accountability and assessment.[3]

Check which responsibilities are yours. Five out of nine more than qualifies you, not only as an expert juggler, but also as an educator able to influence change in your school system. The difficulty or ease in carrying out many administrative tasks depends upon the quality of the culture within the school system. However, in spite of the millions of dollars spent on school improvement, missing from most plans has been the *intentional development of a positive culture* that will support student learning and development. Respected researcher, Michael Fullen, is convinced that the first step to school improvement is to *"re-culture"* the system before attempting to restructure it with new procedures, positions, regulations, curricula or money. It is not the other way around.[4] Now that comes as little surprise to Tribes TLC® school leaders!

Your role as a school leader, particularly if you are a principal or superintendent, is going through an immense change now in the 21st century.

Principals at a conference in Washington State summarized the primary role changes that they face as school leaders today.[5] Three predominant themes are highlighted in a report from their conference:

Moving to Collaboration

Perhaps no more pervasive role change has occurred over the last five to ten years than the expectation that principals should be collaborators and facilitators, rather than authoritarian bosses. As one principal said, "If you are an authoritarian, you may as well get out of the business, because nobody is going to stand for that. I think that is the major change I've seen in the last five to ten years."

Stabilizing the Organization

Principals agree a major concern is simply to maintain stability. They perceive they are being required to manage a stable, disciplined, orderly and compliant system, and at the same time question the curriculum, instruction, decision-making process and quality of student learning. One principal said, "It's a curious situation, kind of like driving with one foot on the brake and one foot on the gas. Things get kind of heated up in that situation." Another principal said, "It's like asking the crew of a 747 to rebuild the airplane while they are flying it."

Then we all agree. We've got to pull the tail off right now and redesign it!

Playing More Roles

In dealing with students, principals see themselves "spending a lot of time being moms, dads, counselors, social agencies and families to these kids." One principal said, "There are all kinds of social issues that were not there when I started thirteen years ago. We got kids into college. Now we get them into treatment. Furthermore, each new popular educational issue usually translates into another role for the principal."

These three significant changes alone, not counting those that you have discovered, call for a new type of leadership and management to handle the multiplicity of issues in today's schools.

No wonder school leaders suffer Excedrin headaches!

> *History despite its wrenching pain cannot be unlived, but if faced with courage need not be lived again.*[6]
>
> —Maya Angelou

WHAT HAVE WE LEARNED

Some of us will recall the panic that happened in 1983 throughout American schools with the release of the U.S. Department of Education report, Nation at Risk. The document about educational failure triggered a leap to establish stricter standards, top-down controls, tougher discipline policies, teacher certification, dress codes, competency statements, and more rules and regulations. The years since then have taken us back and forth on a pendulum between top-down autocratic management and explorations in collaborative planning. During the last ten years schools have tiptoed into site-based management, school-site councils, and teacher empowerment models and pondered how to meet the lofty national directives of *Goals 2000.* Michael Fullen has concluded that neither the top-down nor bottom-up reform strategies have affected the teaching-learning core of schools.

Many desperate school boards, convinced that management methods of the business world could transform schools into efficient systems, hired organizational consultants or sent school leaders to seminars conducted by corporate gurus. Perhaps at one time or another your district was influenced, or still is counting on, one of the approaches described on the next page.[7]

Top-down administrative models are based on *power-over-people* rather than the *empowerment of people.* Compliance rather than creativity and initiative is rewarded. Following the leader becomes more important than following a shared vision; values, ideas and goals for the school community.

Studies indicate that, although the traditional models may for a time alter governance procedures, *teaching and student learning is not affected.*[8] Admitting what does not work with a system takes courage. Ignoring what does not work only guarantees the status quo.

THEORY	BRIEF DESCRIPTION OF MANAGEMENT METHOD
Pyramid	One person at top controls the work of others and holds lower managers accountable for delegated work. The system is dependent upon tight rules and regulations and works well to produce standardized products.
Railroad	Top management controls people who do different jobs in different locations. The work process is standardized with people following tracks from one defined outcome to another. The "one best way" is preached. Following rules is rewarded, not solving problems. In schools, achieving specific objectives for explicit curriculum taught in a specific method is applauded. This is the predominant method of bureaucratic systems.
High Performance	The intention is to de-emphasize hierarchy by inviting staff to make decisions on how to achieve the outcomes previously defined by top management or the school board. The separation of outcome planning from those responsible for implementation too often leaves staff with inadequate resources (materials, adequate training or planning time) to achieve the prescribed outcomes. The high-performance system leads to a calculated focus on curriculum and testing. Teaching to the test becomes the practice throughout the school.

What schools should not do is function as businesses. And school leaders should not function as owners of businesses.[9]

—Peter Senge

WHY ADMINISTRATORS BURN OUT

Ultimately the "follow me" system results in burn out. Jay Conrad Levinson, who ignited the business world with his many books on "guerrilla marketing," urges overworked leaders to leave one century and enter another. He says, "It means embracing new ways of thinking, new ways of working, new ways of living."[10]

Here is the paradigm struggle that both business and educational leaders are facing today.

20TH CENTURY LEADER	21ST CENTURY LEADER
Draconian working hours	Balance between work, family and self
Risks high price for success	Takes sensible risks for humane goals
Autocratic management	Collegial management
Rigid policy and procedures	Flexible and innovative
Top-down control	Shared decision-making
Closed planning system	Open learning system
Focused on long range outcome	Focused on daily process and progress
Works harder	Works smarter
Serious	Playful and creative

The control top-down paradigm is exhausting because it limits the skills and energy of other people. Untapped human resources sentences work or school systems to mediocrity. The 21st century educational leader works smarter by embracing ways to empower many groups and leaders within groups. The empowerment or "calling forth" process of Tribes gives administrators a way to identify and engage a wide range of leaders from the faculty, parent groups and community resource organizations to work for the common good of the students of the school. The administrator must be willing to make a shift in power in meaningful ways, decentralizing planning, problem

It's the Tom Sawyer approach...getting everyone to help paint the fence!

solving and accountability. It is the only way that a strong learning culture can be developed…it must be built collaboratively by a critical mass of people within the system.

Roland Barth, Director of the Principal's Center at Harvard University, urges 21st century school leaders to live "inventive irreverence."[11]

> …conventional wisdom tells school leaders to run their schools to maximize order, minimize dissonance—and thereby to minimize the number of problems that land on the superintendent's desk. As one courageous pair of principals working together toward a goal of interracial understanding found, great learning is often accompanied by great pain—and great dissonance, and even by many phone calls to the central office. They and others discovered that challenging authority, pushing limits, breaking the frame, and "being yourself" in inventive, responsible ways, often accompanied by considerable risk, contributes to profound learning, if not order and comfort, for everyone.

Barth adds that the school leader also needs to be a "reflective practitioner" in order to focus on process… and to be able to admit, "I don't know it all." "To be a learner," he says, "is to admit imperfection. Who inspires more confidence? Who is the better leader? The principal who is learned and wise or the principal who is a lifelong insatiable learner?"

THE HEART OF EFFECTIVE LEADERSHIP

Our work is not about curriculum or a teaching method. It is about nurturing the human spirit with love.[13]

—Ron Miller

Look around! Think of a school leader you consider outstanding. Ten to one you'll say the person is not governed by techniques, but by a desire to bring out the best in the people for whom they are responsible. At the heart of effective leadership whether for managers or teachers is an attitude of genuine caring.[12] They are leaders who...

- Really listen
- Take a caring interest in people under their influence
- Are clear about their expectations
- Are eager to share their own insights and knowledge
- Reinforce strengths and positive behaviors
- Fulfill promises and do not make promises they cannot fulfill
- Are flexible and open to new ideas
- Have a good sense of humor and are enthusiastic
- Are in control of their respective environments

LEADING BY GUIDING

The wise philosopher Confucius once said, "*Superior teacher guides students but does not pull them along. Urges them to go forward by opening the way yet refrains from taking them to the place.*" As ancient as the succinct advice may be, "opening the way" and guiding is the only form of leadership that empowers others to go forward. It is the "leadership for the schoolhouse" of today and tomorrow.[14] It is what this book is all about.

The empowerment way of guiding a school system requires a way "to call forth" a majority of the people in the school community to work toward the common goal of creating a system of educational excellence for the students in their care. People cannot be pushed or pulled into action, but guided by the inclusive process called Tribes, can discover a "wellspring of possibilities" to revitalize learning throughout their whole school community. To guide is to open the gate...

> . . .with two brilliant lanterns pointing to the source, the well-spring of all possibilities." To guide is to lead "the way to the spring, step by step, with wisdom and care.[2]

CHAPTER 2

A People Growing Culture

Harry, the harried principal, was impatient. “Culture! Culture! Re-culture? Forget it, we don’t have time for that stuff. We don’t need a culture.”

Poor Harry doesn’t get it. Every school has a culture, whether good or bad, for its students, teachers and principal.

Culture is the climate, the environment and spirit that permeates everything that goes on within the classrooms, the faculty and other working groups.

Culture is shaped out of the historical patterns that affect how people think and act. This includes the tacit agreements, values, beliefs, ceremonies, rituals, traditions and myths that are passed on year after year in the school.[1] For the most part, the patterns are never recognized or discussed. A great exercise is to have your faculty list some of the unspoken beliefs about teaching, learning and the students of the school. Would you hear any of the following?

> "Those kids just can't learn."
> "As a faculty we don't ask each other for advice."
> "Professional development is always a bore."
> "Behavior on the playground won't improve."
> "We recognize and celebrate students' strengths."

If the staff assumes certain ethnic children cannot learn, one way or another their limiting perceptions undermine the self-image and opportunities for those students. Never doubt that the core beliefs, values, and unspoken relational norms are an active influence on the school system every day.

THE CULTURE THAT KEEPS FISH AND HUMANS SWIMMING

First grade kids can tell us that goldfish cannot live in salt water and ocean fish die in fresh water. Why? Each breed requires its own special environment in order to thrive. This explains why the culture of business organizations, designed to produce standardized products by standardized methods and competition, does not nurture children's development in schools. Healthy and capable people do not come off assembly lines. They cannot be thought of as standardized products. The business of schools is to develop non-standard healthy human beings. That requires a caring cooperative culture that is supportive of the physical, mental, emotional and learning needs of the respective population of children. Discipline policies, curricula, new buildings or an abundance of computers matter little if the school culture centers on institutional mandates and expediency rather than human needs.

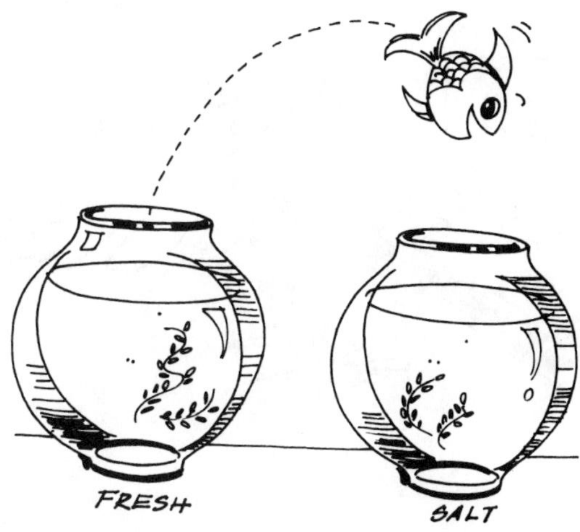

Once the principal and teachers of a school gain an awareness of the nature of the school culture, they have a framework for understanding the forces affecting the school community. This awareness enables them to involve many people in questioning how well the patterns support learning and development. Educators need to realize that positive school cultures correlate strongly with increased student achievement and motivation, and with teacher productivity and satisfaction.[2]

LOOKING AT THE COMPONENTS

Jerome Bruner, respected cognitive and developmental psychologist from Harvard, Oxford and New York University, writes:

> What is needed in America—as in most countries of the developed world—is not simply a renewal of the skills that make a country a better competitor in the world markets, but a renewal and reconsideration of what is called *school culture.* On the basis of what we have learned in recent years about human learning—it is best when it is *participatory, proactive, communal, collaborative and given over to constructive meanings rather than receiving them.* We do even better at teaching science, math, and languages in such schools than in more traditional ones.[3]

Bruner asserts: "It is our ideas that need restructuring, before we can redesign our institutions." Contrast two schools that regard student learning differently. The one set of beliefs can be considered "life-liberating" and the other "life-limiting."[4]

Those of you who are leaders in schools using the process of Tribes, will recognize that the process incorporates the components for an ideal learning culture.

LIFE-LIBERATING	LIFE LIMITING
All children are capable of high achievement.	Only the bright few can achieve at a high level.
You do not have to understand everything the first time around.	Speed is what counts. Faster is smarter.
Consistent effort is the determinant of success.	Inborn intelligence is the determinant.
Mistakes help one learn.	Mistakes are a sign of weakness.
Good students work together, and solicit help from one another.	Competition is necessary to bring out the best in our students.

Creating a positive school culture to support human learning depends upon people agreeing how they will connect to and respect each other. Clear positive agreements need to replace unclear negative norms. Shared beliefs on student development and learning, core teaching concepts and a common vision for all students of the school is essential. Each day we need to ask, "Is the overall climate of our school supportive, challenging and caring?"

IDEAL LEARNING CULTURE	THE TRIBES PROCESS
Communal	Builds community and inclusion for all Uses cooperative learning Transfers responsibility to groups Promotes caring and sharing Celebrates community learning
Participatory	Reaches all students through meaningful participation Uses interactive strategies Encourages peer leadership
Proactive	Uses positive agreements to assure a caring culture Reaches students of multiple intelligences, abilities and cultures Trains teachers to use brain compatible methods and communication
Collaborative	Invites influence Uses consensus strategies Promotes teacher collegiality
Constructive Meaning	Involves students in research and teaching content of interest Uses student planning groups

Let's face it. A non-tribes school has a lot of pretending going on!

MAKING LIFE EASIER

The good news is that the daily life of school leaders changes dramatically by using the Tribes community building process. It doesn't happen overnight, but with time and persistence in establishing a whole new way of "learning and being together" the culture of a school becomes transformed. A group of Tribes TLC® principals and other administrators made the following list to highlight the changes that they experienced:

THE NON-TRIBES SCHOOL	THE TRIBES TLC® SCHOOL
Me (the lonely administrator)	We (the collegial community)
Top-down decision-making	Shared decision-making and leadership
Lack of support	Enthusiastic support from staff and parents
Tremendous pressure alone	Shared responsibility
Disconnected people	Connected groups and relationships
Back stabbing/no trust	Caring, kindness and trust
Lack of verification	Appreciation from staff
Problem based	Solution based
Competition and power games	Cooperation and honesty
Always "up and on"	Permission to say "I don't know. I need your help."
Curriculum centered	Student-centered
Unclear goals, norms, and teaching concepts	Clear shared goals, agreements, and pedological principles
Decision-making in the parking lot	Decision-making in staff meetings
Stand alone in times of crisis	Community stands together

TWO CULTURES—
WHICH ONE IS YOUR SCHOOL?

The two columns on the previous page illustrating two very different school cultures, are contrasted in a Rand Corporation study.[5] The left-hand column could well describe "zoned" schools, and the other column "focused" schools. *Focused schools* concentrate on *student outcomes* and have *strong social contracts and positive cultures.* Principals, teachers, parents and students pull together to achieve clear goals, and give their personal support to the school community. In contrast, *zoned schools* focus primarily on delivering curriculum, programs, and following procedures. They usually have unclear cultures and social norms. Studies indicate that students of zoned schools score well below the scores of focused-school students. The latter also have a higher level of school pride and state that their school has a good learning environment.

The process of Tribes builds focused schools. The Tribes agreements work as strong social contracts. The learned social skills that are used throughout school classes and meetings sustain a positive culture. The *community building process* based on inclusion prevents a lot of problems for management.

Sounds great! How do we get all this to happen?

That's what our discussion will be about...how you, the school administrator, can gracefully guide and share leadership with many others by using the caring process of Tribes at all levels of the school system.[6] It requires collaborative skills coupled with vision and heart. It means *guiding rather than directing* and *following in order to lead.*

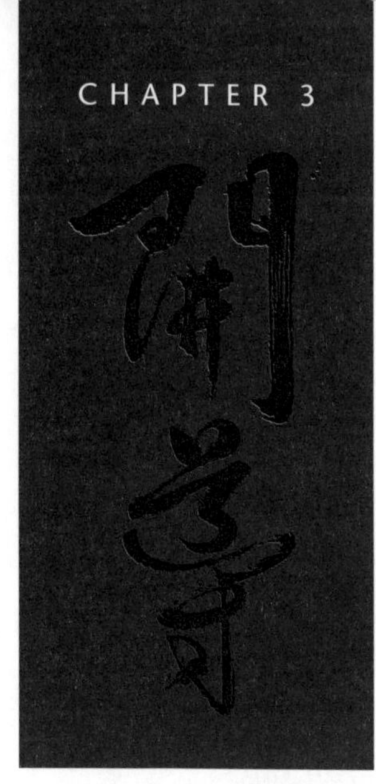

THE ROOTS OF LEADERSHIP—BUILDING COMMUNITY AND COLLEGIALITY

It is this quest for community toward which the roots of school leadership must be directed.[1]

—Thomas Sergiovanni

What happens when the sense of belonging and community is missing from the school? What happens if the adults in the school never talk about higher purposes or mission or meaning in any intentional way with each other or with the students? What if teachers and students never talk about what they are trying to achieve with each other and with students? What is the likely result of this lack of shared purpose?

We intentionally create a dysfunctional school. I believe many schools skip over community building, i.e.: creating a shared purpose, just to get on with the practical and time-devouring busi-ness of school—classes, subject matter, discipline, scheduling, grading, and paperwork. As adults we can still function—though not joyfully—within such a setting. Our students, however, sense our fragmentation and lack of unity and purpose. They have neither

> the maturity or experience to deal with the conflicting purposes and expectations which swirl around them. Many times they feel lost and overwhelmed. School for them is not safe and secure, but arbitrary and pointless, run by adults all on a game plan that they are not allowed to understand. —Judi Fenton, Principal

TO IMPROVE EDUCATION

If indeed we are to improve education in America, schools must be transformed into inclusive caring communities that focus on human development and learning rather than bureaucratic expediency. Thomas Sobol, professor of Education at Teacher's College, Columbia University, reports that when a gathering of "beleaguered school superintendents" were asked to discuss their greatest concern, they lamented the decline of community in America—and the role of the public schools in creating and sustaining community. They were concerned that setting lofty standards will not by itself address the problem of creating the community needed for attaining high standards.[2]

The work of respected educators such as James Comer (Yale School Development Program), Deborah Meier (Central Park Schools), Thomas Sergiovanni (Trinity University) and innumerable others affirm the need for community.

> Schools must be communities where children feel comfortable, valued and secure.[3] —James Comer

> Establishing community in our school, meaningful relationships between adults and students was as important as all the changes made in teaching, curriculum and assessment.[4] —Deborah Meier

> Nearly everyone agrees that our schools and our society have a connections problem. And nearly everyone agrees that one way to renew connections is to help schools to become caring communities.[5] —Thomas Sergiovanni

WHAT IS COMMUNITY?

Community is defined in many ways. A good first stepfor a staff or parent group is to set aside time to share cherished moments when they felt a sense of belonging and being valued in a group living the essence of "community."

Educator Thomas Likona writes:

> To build a sense of community is to create a group that extends to others the respect one has for oneself...to come to know one another as individuals, to respond and care about one another, to feel a sense of membership and accountability to the group.[6]

Building on studies of community in work and school settings, the Office of Educational Research and Improvement identified ten elements that characterize adult-student relations in schools considered true communities. Within the schools people have...

- A shared vision
- A sense of purpose
- Shared values
- An incorporation of diversity
- Open communication
- Active participation
- Caring
- Trust
- Teamwork
- Respect and recognition

The weakening or absence of these attributes more often than not accompanies program failure.

Those schools consciously working at strengthening the elements are, in the view of the researchers, building the necessary foundation for excellence.[7]

Author John McKnight points out five indicators of community:

Capacity Communities are built upon recognizing the whole depth, the strengths, weaknesses, and the unique capacities of each member.

Collective effort Communities share responsibility to achieve goals for the common good, and engage the diversity of individual talents and skills to do so.

Informality Transactions of value are based on consideration; care and affection take place spontaneously.

Stories Reflection upon individual and community experiences provides knowledge about truth, relationships and future direction.

Celebration Activities incorporate celebration, parties, and social events. The line between work and play is blurred as people enjoy both at once.

McKnight also has said, "You will know you are in a community if you often hear laughter and singing. You will know when you are in a bureaucracy if you hear the silence of long halls and the intonations of formal meetings."[8]

CAN YOU DO IT ALONE?

> We cannot endure the expectations and pressure of reform without a trusting team...a system of support, a solid school community. This is where Tribes fits in.
>
> —Judi Fenton, Principal

Sure, build community! But how?

Although it is the principal who sets the tone and carries the ultimate responsibility, only the naive believe the job can be done alone. To develop a caring school community a leader must have a trusting team, namely the faculty. The big question is how can a collegial support system be developed among teachers when traditionally they see themselves simply as captains of their isolated classrooms? More often than not, they may relate briefly to two or three other teachers in their grade level or in the faculty lunchroom. Occasional discussions typically deal with the three C's: children, curriculum and complaints. It has been estimated that teachers spend up to 90% of their time with students, and do not have the time nor inclination to work together on school-wide issues. A teacher who has five years teaching experience has been in school a minimum of 7,440 teaching hours, has been with other adults (including their supervisors) less than 1% of the time, or 74 hours. Faculty meetings for the most part consist of listening to announcements with minimal interaction among colleagues.[9]

Recognizing that the isolation of teachers from each other inhibits collegiality and professional development many administrators count on one-shot workshops and outside speakers to talk, train, or entertain the staff. Teachers may also be urged to attend unrelated college courses. Thomas Hoerr describes the problem well...

Growing professionally is too often defined as going somewhere to take a course or attend a workshop. Is it any wonder that teachers fly out of town in order to sit together and talk about what is happening in the hall outside their rooms?[10]

Virtually every profession but ours protects times during the day for its members to work together as learners.[12]

—Thomas Hoerr

SCHOOL-WIDE PROFESSIONAL DEVELOPMENT

Studies indicate that when schools become places for teachers to learn, they also become schools on the way to improvement. School policies need to enable schools to accomplish the following goals:

- Redesign school structures to support teacher learning and collaboration on practice
- Rethink schedules and staffing patterns to create blocks of time for teachers to plan and work together
- Organize the school into small, collaborative groups (yes, tribes)
- Make it possible for teachers to think in terms of shared problems, not “my classroom” or “my subject”
- Consider using peer review rather than standard hierarchical supervision, and
- Include everyone in a school community, such as principals, counselors, parents, in creating a shared purpose (i.e., the tribes community process).[11]

Although the connection between on-going professional development and student achievement is largely recognized, the allocation of sufficient time and resources may initially be perceived as so impossible that the imperative for professional development is discredited and minimized.

Please tell all the educators whom you know about one wise Superintendent, who did prioritize the reallocation of time and resources for professional development, and as a result was nominated by the American Association of School Administrators as one of four national "Superintendent of the Year" finalists. Speaking to the association, he said:

> What got me here was the quality staff we have in our district. Everything in our district revolves around professional development. Teachers have without question the hardest job in America. The classroom is dramatically different than it was just five years ago and teachers need more skills than five years ago. $7 million of our district's $120 million now is spent on some form of staff development. I am convinced that every administrator must allocate about 20 days per year to staff development.[13]

The good news is that a growing number of educators and school boards are recognizing that while other reforms may be needed, better learning for more children ultimately relies on the competency and collegiality of the teachers within the school.

THERE IS A MAP!

Our imperative is to establish *a new set of three C's: caring culture, collegiality and community.* The phrase *learning community* reached the ears of educators as Peter Senge's fine book, *The Fifth Discipline, The Art and Practice of the Learning Community* came into prominence.[14] For educators it added to the growing consensus on WHY and WHAT needs to happen to improve teaching and learning in schools. The HOW to develop a school learning community has remained vague…unless you are a school leader who learned (probably from colleagues) that the Tribes Learning Community (TLC®) process does it. Moreover, if you have a copy of that book called *Reaching All by Creating Tribes Learning Communities,* you are probably familiar with the how-to-do-it map, and may be well on your way.[16]

Up until now you may have considered that the Tribes Trail Map on the next page primarily illustrates how teachers can build cooperative learning groups within classrooms. Look Again! Now you need to perceive the Map as a way to transform the whole school system into a community for learning. This time think about the theory and concepts as applied to adult groups instead of classrooms of students. This time see yourself as the facilitator guiding people along the community building trail.

It may take a village to raise a child, but it takes a community to raise a school system to excellence.

—Jeanne Gibbs

The same training that your teachers have had can be used to lead and manage the school community. The same process and agreements are used within meetings with your faculty, support staff, site-councils, resource agencies, parent volunteers, bus drivers and cooks. Everyone needs a sense of belonging (inclusion) and value (influence). Everyone longs for the spirit of working together as a community.

It's mind-boggling to realize what Thomas Sergiovanni, author of the great book *Leadership for the Schoolhouse* suggests when he states: "The role of a school leader is simply to help the community problem solve." It means that the leader does not solve

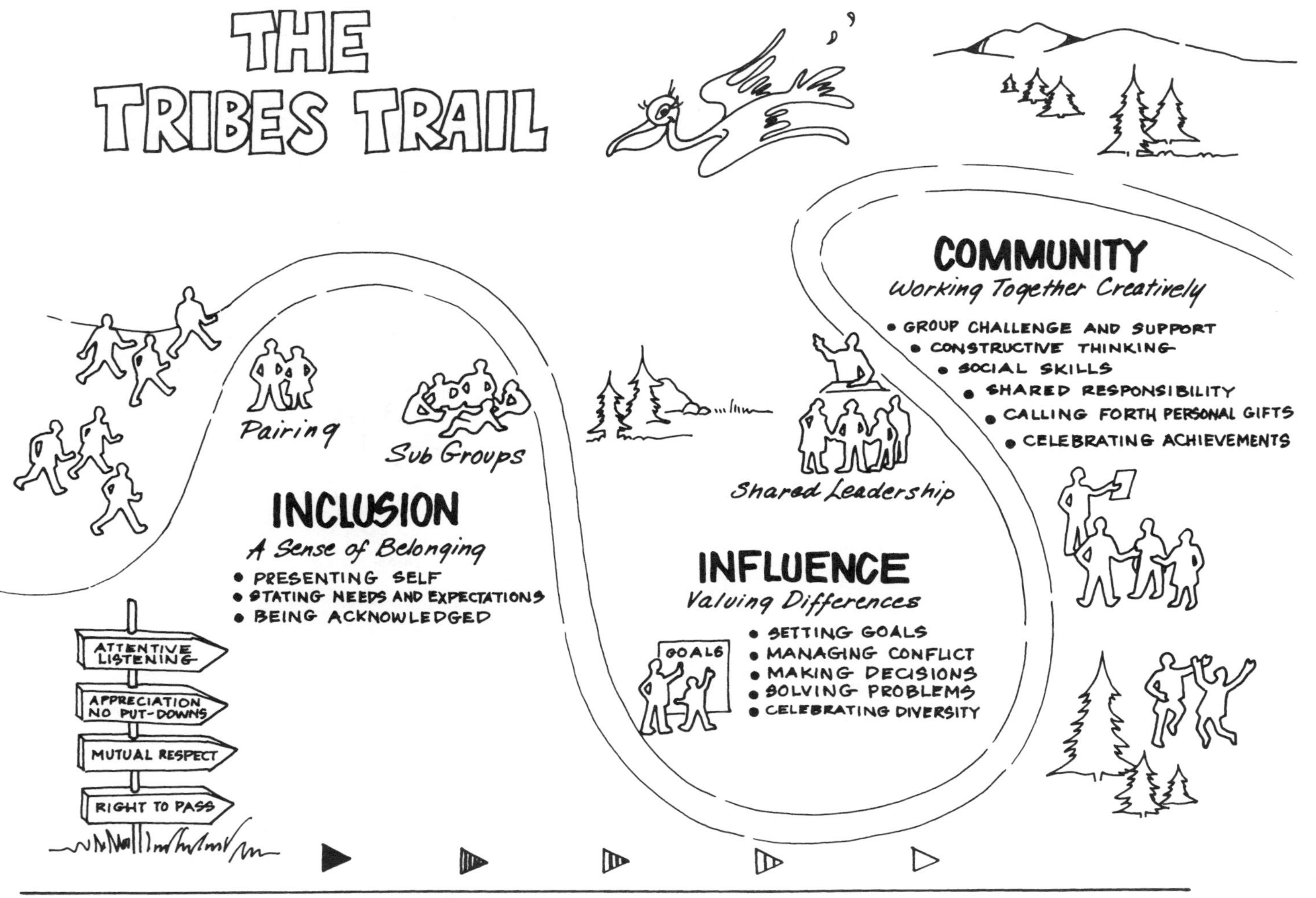
THE TRIBES TRAIL
Pairing
Sub Groups
INCLUSION
A Sense of Belonging
• PRESENTING SELF
• STATING NEEDS AND EXPECTATIONS
• BEING ACKNOWLEDGED
ATTENTIVE LISTENING
APPRECIATION NO PUT-DOWNS
MUTUAL RESPECT
RIGHT TO PASS
Shared Leadership
INFLUENCE
Valuing Differences
• SETTING GOALS
• MANAGING CONFLICT
• MAKING DECISIONS
• SOLVING PROBLEMS
• CELEBRATING DIVERSITY
GOALS
COMMUNITY
Working Together Creatively
• GROUP CHALLENGE AND SUPPORT
• CONSTRUCTIVE THINKING
• SOCIAL SKILLS
• SHARED RESPONSIBILITY
• CALLING FORTH PERSONAL GIFTS
• CELEBRATING ACHIEVEMENTS
FACILITATOR'S ROLE: TRANSFER RESPONSIBILITY TO GROUP

or carry all the problems. Trustworthy groups work on solutions and help to take action. It's the Tom Sawyer method! And facilitating the process of Tribes is the proven step-by-step way to do it.

The best way to control your cow is not to control.
Offer, instead, a large spacious meadow.
—Confucius

What is the first big difference you may notice in your school?

A principal from a Midwest state phoned the Tribes office one day to say,

> People certainly were right! Sure, I guessed Tribes was going to work with the kids. But there was something I didn't quite believe. It's really true...tardies have gone down, attendance is up, and now there are hardly any conflicts or problems. And, Jeanne, that's just with the teachers!

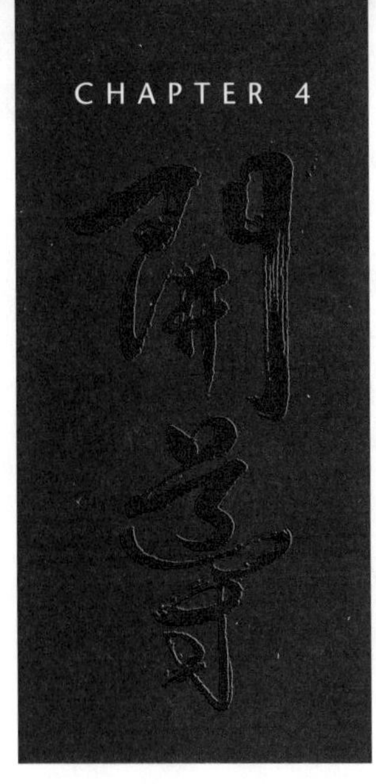

CHAPTER 4

INITIATING THE JOURNEY

> When I first became Superintendent I knew our need was to build community throughout the district. Every classroom, every faculty member, every administrator needs to feel special…to be valued for the different talents they bring. It sounds so simple. I believed if we could do that, we would resolve 99% of the problems that we have in education. Gradually, I became convinced that this process called Tribes was a way to build the community to do this.
>
> —Aileen Hokama, Superintendent
> Central Oahu District, Hawaii[1]

Within every school or district there are some folks who have a vision that their school system can be dramatically improved if a critical mass of others become convinced of the same possibility. "Yes," Superintendent Hokama continued in our interview, "it would be nice if people would just accept and believe that building a new culture and community with the Tribes process would be invaluable. Many teachers and principals still clinging to being authorities fear losing control. One way or another, they have to get involved in the practice (experience the process)...though they do not have to believe right away."

ONE DISTRICT'S ADOPTION STORY

The Tribes process has never stayed neatly just in classrooms. In time the caring culture, agreements and energy spills over into the faculty room, parent conferences, and district meetings. Because Tribes is not a curriculum to be taught but a process to be lived, once experienced, it is more easily adopted and internalized. District decision makers and reluctant leaders may not join the trail right away, but as Aileen Hokama advises, involve them in the practice one way or another. Even the most remote can be melted with inclusion and appreciation. They also need to gain some knowledge of the benefits, but do not have to jump aboard right away. There is one more big plus factor to count on. Most people evaluate an innovation, not on the basis of scientific research by experts, but on the subjective evaluations of near peers who have already adopted the innovation.[2]

The spread of Tribes to 3,000 educators and 70 trainers in Hawaii came about in that way over a period of four years. The innovation began when one Central Oahu District principal, Nancy Latham, experienced a Tribes overview workshop at a Western

Center for Drug Free Schools conference in Portland, Oregon. She became convinced that Tribes would give her students, primarily from military-based families, the sense of belonging and caring community that they needed so badly. She shared what she had learned with her teachers who also recognized the benefit that the inclusive caring process would be. Training was arranged and implementation begun. Soon teachers began to talk to teachers in other schools. Principals talked to principals. In time, Superintendent Hokama became aware that two schools were experiencing some positive results. She states, "If something is working in our schools, our job is to make certain we can translate it into practice for other schools. Opportunities for training and networking have to occur." That meant that the District had to designate an educational coordinator to guide the system-wide strategies. It came as no surprise that innovator Nancy Latham was invited to handle the task at the district level. A bit later we'll review sequences of networking and professional development strategies. The Superintendent concludes that:

A sense of community is a perception that members have of belonging and being important to each other.[3]

—James Comer

> This was a grass-root effort at its best. Before the District had Tribes, we would decide from the top how to manage everything. At times we may have wondered how to engage the schools to do what we wanted them to do. Yet somehow we knew we had to get away from the top-down paradigm. Just like little kids, we kept band-aiding rather than recognizing that the band-aids had become the system. Tribes gave us a way to set up

> parameters to operate and to deal well with the diversity of people. Now people sit down and talk problems through with colleagues before it comes to this office. We're more productive as a unit. Tribes has allowed us to build community and trust.

GAINING COMMITMENT

Let's assume that you have decided, as have hundreds of other school leaders, that the Tribes process is the best way to support student learning and development in your school. How can you gain commitment from the teachers of your school? Studies on how a critical mass of people adopt an innovation point to a sequence of stages that the group must be led through. Introducing the new school culture of Tribes, like any other innovation within a system, is met with varying degrees of enthusiasm, doubt and hope. Here at Tribes headquarters, we are sometimes asked how long it takes for a majority of teachers in a school to make the Tribes TLC® process their own. School leaders also ask how long it takes to transform a school into a caring collaborative community. Our reply is that it depends upon the rate at which people move through these predictable stages.[4]

1. Knowledge — Some decision-makers or leaders gain an understanding and perceive the benefits of the new process or method.

2. Persuasion — The early adopters (peers) tell others.

3. Decision	People agree to participate in an activity that leads to making a choice (i.e.: hear a presentation, discuss with peers, watch a video, visit demonstration classrooms).
4. Implementation	People take steps to learn (training, support and peer-coaching).
5. Confirmation	People give each other support and reinforcement.

These stages are *what* needs to happen. *How* to involve others happens through use of the Tribes community building process. It's all about *inclusion, inclusion, inclusion!*

As Superintendent Hokama states, "one way or another they have to get involved in the practice." They have to experience the process even as you begin to guide the way.

A helpful scenario

First, a small group needs to gain *knowledge.* They need to learn about and recognize the benefits that the process can bring to their school or district.

- Invite 6–8 open-minded teachers to discuss and list the needs of teachers (discipline, teaching methods, professional development, school climate, collegiality, etc.). Use inclusion, listening, appreciation.

- Share how the process of Tribes could address these needs; provide information (Tribes book, videotape, brochure, Tribes goals and objectives).*

---

*Contact CenterSource Systems for information and presentation materials.

- Invite the group to visit Tribes classrooms in a nearby school, or arrange for each person to talk by phone to teachers and school leaders using the process.

- Invite the group to debrief (reflect) on what they learned; make lists of the benefits they perceive of using Tribes in the school.*

- Invite all teachers to a community meeting led by two teachers of the first group. Have everyone sit in a large community circle, use an *inclusion* strategy (i.e., what would make my teaching day easier), the Tribes agreements reflection and appreciation. Provide information about Tribes and facilitate discussion in small groups on how the components of Tribes would address their needs (again use *inclusion, reflection and appreciation*).*

Making a decision to implement Tribes and to have training may best be the content of a second meeting, depending upon the readiness of the faculty to decide. Key to the decision for implementation is the first group talking to peers in leadership roles.

THE TRIBES TLC® LEADERSHIP MAP

Although we know that you are familiar with the Tribes Trail Map contained in the previous chapter, the map in this chapter has been redrawn to illustrate how the Tribes process is used throughout multiple levels of a school system.

It shows the familiar three community building steps: *inclusion, influence and community* that you

*Contact CenterSource Systems for information and presentation materials.

The Tribes Leadership Map

for Re-culturing and Building Community Throughout a School System

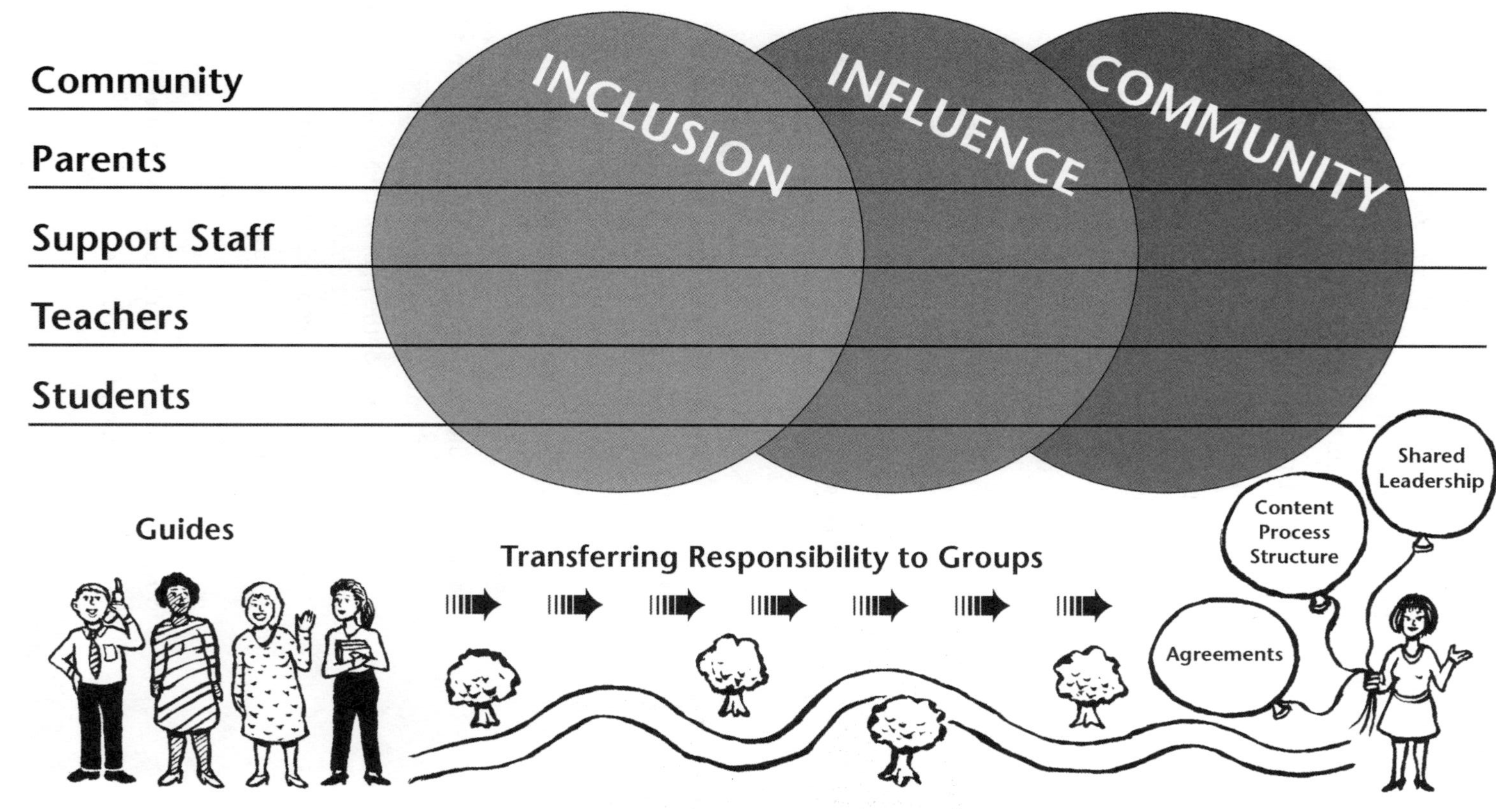

will implement to reculture and manage the school community. If you turn back to the previous page, that's you over there on the right hand side holding three balloons which are essential components for any kind of meeting, class, conference, celebration or gathering that you plan to do. The components are the Tribes Agreements, Shared Leadership and the integration of content, process and structure. The latter balloon, (content, process, structure) is extremely important.

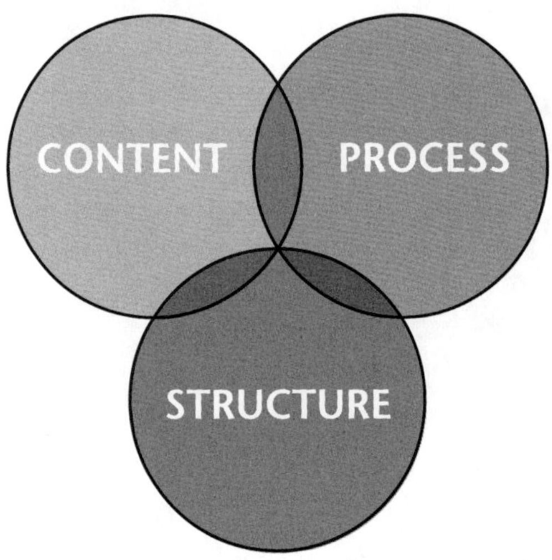

Content the problem to be solved, the information to be learned, the theme, idea or concept to be discussed, the plan or decision to be made

Process the timed sequence of strategies (inclusion, influence, community building) and events that lead to the goal to be achieved

Structure the group configurations for meeting (community circle, tribes, dyads, triads etc.)

Just like a three-legged stool, all three are needed for a successful event. Think about any one or two without the other:

- One person is talking content in straight-row seating: the structure limits inclusion and influence and forces the speaker to keep talking. The meeting is speaker-centered, authoritarian and loses listeners attention. Content is all, process and structure are ignored.
- Random groups doing energizers or active strategies: no goals are cited; no content; little process awareness. Structure and content are ignored.
- People are in large circle discussing a problem; no inclusion, no stated objective or agreements. Process is ignored and the structure, though a circle, does not assure inclusion or build community.

When these examples are spotted in classrooms, you can conclude the Tribes process is not happening. Teachers who just count off kids into task groups (structure) and do not allow time for inclusion, reflection and appreciation are not really implementing the cooperative learning/community building process of Tribes. Moreover, the content to be learned will not be learned or worked on productively.

That third balloon on the map is *shared leadership.* You may have worried up until now that you would be the lonely guide carrying the full responsibility. Remember Tom Sawyer watching many people paint the fence! As you move along the trail guiding groups throughout the faculty, support staff, parent and other school populations, many leaders will emerge. For now we've noted them on the map as *guides*. They could be three teachers of the faculty who help to plan faculty meetings or who do classroom demonstrations and coaching. They could be a team of four parents who train other parents to plan and facilitate classroom parent tribes, or groups for "Back-to-School Night." They all help to facilitate the process... sharing leadership, planning and integrating those components (balloons) throughout all of the meetings, events and gatherings that they help to plan in the

respective groups (faculty, support staff, parent etc.). No, facilitators are not hired. They come forward. They are the people who recognize the potential benefit of the Tribes process for their school, and are committed to having their own system of peers take an active part in developing a caring community school culture. Flying high on the map is our pelican friend, Reflection, reminding everyone to take time out to reflect on how things are working each step of the way. Keep in mind our new Tribes saying,

> It may take a village to raise a child,
> but it takes a community to raise a school system.

CHAPTER 5

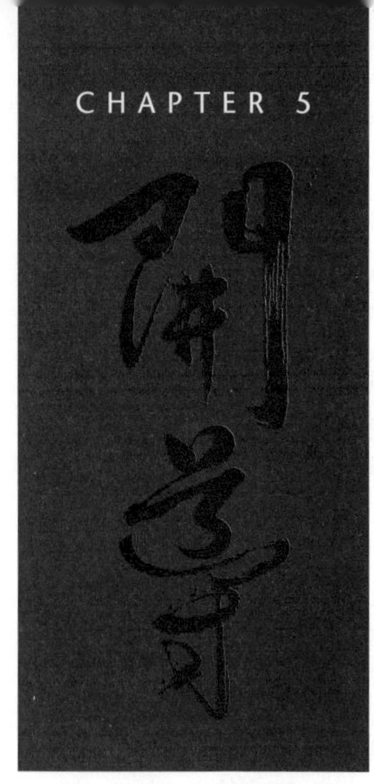

Creating the Culture

The next two chapters are the "how to do it" chapters you have been waiting for. (Oops, that's a preposition at the end of a sentence. Yes, I know, but want this dialogue with you to be informal.) The content of the two chapters comes out of the wealth of experiences that other Tribes TLC® school leaders have had, and is based directly on the same theory, framework and strategies used in classrooms. These chapters will guide you further along the Tribes Trail . . .

- to create the caring community culture
- to sustain the culture over many years in a school or district, and
- to extend the culture throughout the many levels and population groups of a school community.

Where does it all start?
With faculty training, of course.

PARTICIPATE IN TRIBES TLC® TRAINING

Creating the new culture within your school begins by joining your teachers in Tribes TLC® professional development training. The concepts and learning experience of the CenterSource Systems twenty-four hour Basic course is the foundation for re-culturing the school. If you have already participated in training, you know that it develops collegiality and a common language for teaching, relating and managing the school as a Tribes Learning Community. It is "a new way of learning and being together."

During the training, teachers and school leaders begin to realize that the traditional direct-teaching and top-down management structure is the trap that inhibits collegiality, trust and collaboration. A paragraph in the big Tribes book cites how the use of the Tribes TLC® process affects teachers:

> The new pattern of interaction changes the role of the *teacher* in a dramatic way. *Teachers* now see themselves as learners, facilitators, researchers and designers of *curricula.* When *teachers* work in collegial groups their inherent isolation disappears.[1]

Substituting the word *principal* for *teacher* and the word *meetings* for *curricula* gives a picture of the change that can be realized for administrators.

Just as in a Tribes cooperative learning classroom, the school leader initiates staff meetings with inclusion strategies, and in time decentralizes planning and problem solving to faculty groups (tribes). Just as teachers see new creative energy and support among students, administrators see the same among teachers. Just as a teacher's use of the Tribes process opens up a new climate of respect in the classroom, the same happens with the faculty. Moreover, perhaps for the first time, the teaching staff will come to recognize and be able to share their wealth of untapped knowledge, skills and creativity. The spirit of collegiality, key to professional development and school improvement, is a contagious people-to-people phenomenon that energizes a school community like a new song.

The Tribes TLC® training prepares everyone to be *facilitators of learning . . . to be process guides* who help to introduce the caring culture to the many groups within the school system.

FACILITATE THE TRIBES COMMUNITY BUILDING PROCESS

Know that by using the inclusive caring TLC® process, your life as an administrator will be more fun! Count on having fewer disenchanted folks pounding on your door. The basic theory of Tribes pertains to adults as well as students.

> If a person does not feel included, he or she will create his own inclusion by grabbing influence—attracting attention, creating a controversy, demanding power or withdrawing into passive belligerence.

"Whoa!" you say, "I've had a few incidents and folks like that. There was that caucus of teachers, the special education parents, the upset school board member, and that district program coordinator."

In the same way that teachers using the Tribes process have fewer behavioral problems; principals and even beleaguered superintendents also will enjoy mellower moments once they learn to use the inclusive process to lead the school community. Building community throughout the many groups and levels within a school system also means facilitating the stages of *inclusion, influence and community.* It might be helpful for you to review pages 70–78 in Chapter 6 of the book *Reaching All by Creating Tribes Learning Communities.* If you truly want your school to be transformed into a caring community culture, you will not only be modeling the concepts in planned meetings, but living them with the many people who daily come your way.

FOR NEWCOMERS

Let's be honest now. Perhaps one way or another you picked up this book from another school leader's desk, and now you want to know more about the Tribes TLC® professional development training. We urge you either to:

- Set up a luncheon date with your friend, after admitting you have this book
- Check out the Professional Development pages 405–407 in the book, *Reaching All by Creating Tribes Learning Communities*
- Or phone CenterSource Systems (800-810-1701). They can send materials, provide other information and names of others using Tribes.

As discussed in the last chapter, considering an innovation for your school or district begins with gaining knowledge and talking to peers.

Finding Funding

The phone rings at the Tribes office. Sarah Jones, Principal in Harvest, Iowa says,

> Ah, yes, our whole staff wants to be trained in Tribes next year. The district is supportive if I can identify funding.

The staff member at CenterSource replies,

> Congratulations, Sarah! It's no big problem. Trot back to your district office and first let them know that just about any and all Federal and State funds can be used as well as funding from several foundations for Tribes TLC® staff development.

Schools need to specify the appropriate goals and objectives to be achieved through a particular source of funding and identify the positive process of Tribes as the way the objectives will be achieved. Tribes is the implementation process.

In addition to citing the Tribes TLC® participatory process as a way to achieve various categorical program objectives, schools can secure funding by defining how the salient components of Tribes TLC® address critical student and school needs:

- Teaching and learning refusal skills
- Conflict resolution
- Respect for cultural and racial diversity
- Cooperative learning
- Violence prevention
- Youth leadership
- School reform
- School climate

Following are some of the many sources of funding that are being used by schools in the United States.

Sources for Funding the Tribes Process through Staff Development

FEDERAL SOURCES IN THE UNITED STATES

US Department of Education

www.ed.gov/fund

The U.S. Department of Education administers numerous grant programs. This site links to grant and contract information, department applications and guidelines, and the Federal Register of grant opportunities: www.ed.gov/news/fedregister

Health and Human Services

http://dhhs.gov

This site contains multiple funding opportunities that will stretch your imagination for the use of the Tribes process—from HeadStart to Aging Services.

Substance Abuse and Mental Health Services Administration (SAMHSA)

www.samhsa.gov

This agency is charged with improving the quality and availability of prevention, treatment, and rehabilitation services. SAMHSA oversees the funding opportunities that are offered by:

Center for Substance Abuse Prevention (CSAP)
http://prevention.samhsa.gov
Center for Mental Health Services (CMHS)
http://mentalhealth.samhsa.gov/cmhs

US Department of Justice

www.usdoj.gov

This agency collaborates with the US Department of Education in offering grant opportunities related to safe schools, violence/ bullying prevention, and delinquency prevention through the:

Office of Juvenile Justice Delinquency
Prevention (OJJDP)
http://ojjdp.ncjrs.org

STATE AND LOCAL FUNDING SOURCES

State dollars are available for staff development in specific areas such as gifted and talented education, special education, vocational education, character education, and school reform. You need to check directly with the Department of Education in your state for additional information on grants that are available.

Local Funding sources can range from the PTA to crime prevention agencies and service clubs. Talk to civic groups, banks and community organizations about the need for students to have collaborative skills for the world of work. No doubt, all will join in telling stories about folks that relate well to computers in isolated cubicles, but do not get along with fellow workers. The majority of people who lose their jobs do so because of their inability to work collaboratively with others—not because they lack the necessary job skills. When local business people learn that the Tribes TLC® process teaches the necessary skills for the workplace and life relationships, their check books will come out!

FOUNDATIONS, CORPORATIONS

A search of the internet gives a number of foundations and corporations that are willing to fund projects such as Tribes. We have found several generic sources, which we think you will find very useful.

The Foundation Center

www.foundationcenter.org

The Foundation Center is an independent nonprofit information-clearing house on grants available in the United States. This site includes online training in grantseeking, proposal writing, and funding research.

The Finance Project

www.financeproject.org

The Finance Project provides information on how to use federal funds for a variety of programs, including in-school and after-school programs.

NEA Foundation

www.neafoundation.org

The NEA Foundation provides a variety of funding opportunities for school programs and professional development. Tribes TLC is featured in the NEA publication, *CARE: Culture, Abilities, Resilience, Effort: Strategies for Closing the Achievement Gaps.*

CANADIAN FUNDING OPPORTUNITIES

Government of Canada

www.canada.gc.ca contains information on Canada's governmental departments and agencies.

Foundation Search

Funding opportunities can also be found by visiting: www.foundationsearch.ca

AUSTRALIA AND INTERNATIONAL

Funds Net Services
www.fundsnetservices.com
Search on *Australia* or *International* for funding opportunities available in various countries.

If you discover some helpful links for funding in your area, please let us know so that we can share the information with others.

If you are applying for funding to implement or intensify the use of the Tribes Learning Community process, feel free to contact CenterSource or visit the Tribes website at www.tribes.com for supporting documentation, including research and model program status.

MODELING THE PROCESS

Creating the new culture means Inclusion! Inclusion! Inclusion! Take a moment now and turn back to the Tribes Trail Map in Chapter Three. *Living inclusion* means taking the time to offer each person an opportunity . . .

- To present who she or he is (special qualities, interests and feelings)
- To express hopes and expectations, and
- To be acknowledged as having been heard and appreciated.

The words in the theme song of that old television program "Cheers" express the longing for a place "where everybody knows my name." One Tribes principal shared how each morning she would stand at the front door of the school greeting as many teachers and students as she could by name. "Happy to see you today, Marilyn." "I'm glad to see you this morning, Juan." Her practice was contagious. Teachers began doing the same, welcoming students by name at the doors of their rooms.

Good morning, Michael, nice to see you.
Hi, Laurie, good job on the prom committee. Hello, Brooke, Sean . . .

Model inclusion as much as possible with parents and staff:

"Thelma, I'd appreciate you sharing your insight with the faculty today."

"How wonderful that you have taught calculus, Mrs. Gonzales."

"Your organizational ability, Don, is a very important resource for the parent program."

Address people by name, speak to the strengths that you perceive, and be genuine in affirmation and appreciation. That, of course, is the way not only of inclusion but of building resilience in people and systems!

THE FIRST FACULTY MEETING

A good first step in initiating the new Tribes culture within the faculty is to invite two or three teachers to help plan and assume some leadership of the meetings. This shift immediately moves you off the top-of-the-pyramid position and into a collaborative structure.

Remember that the three essential components *content, process and structure* must be integrated for any Tribes event whether a meeting or classroom learning experience.

The *content* is whatever the faculty meeting is to be about: planning back-to-school night, discussion of district policy, calendar announcements, etc. This is *what* needs to be accomplished in the meeting.

Rather than list the items as "the agenda," it is far better to refer to them as *meeting objectives*. Notice the difference that it makes in expectations.

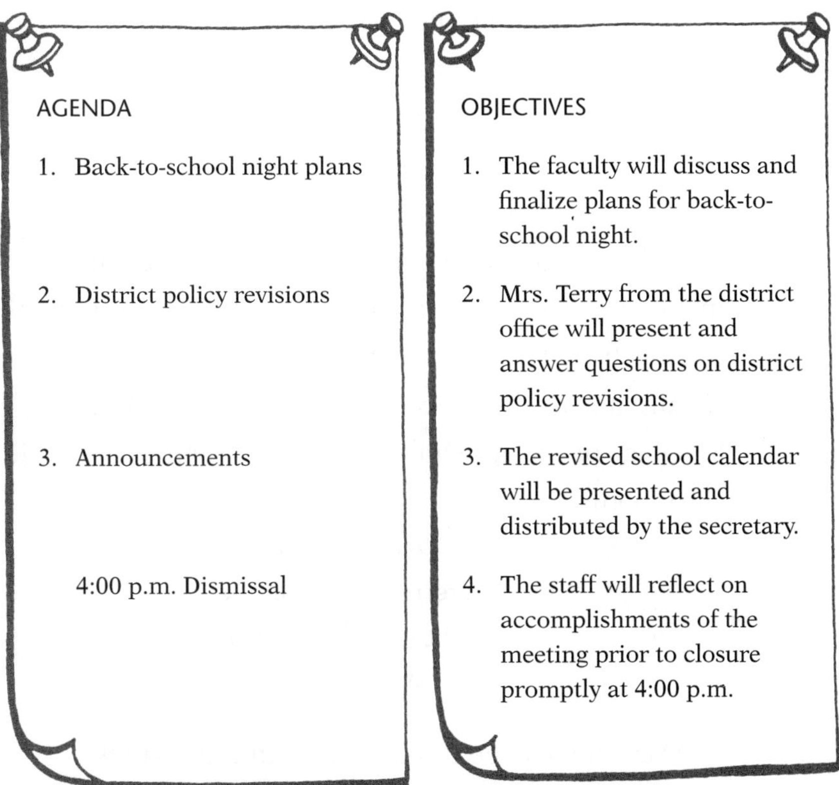

Rephrasing the agenda as objectives conveys that the tasks indeed will be accomplished. It is the same as having teachers write clear objectives for a lesson plan, and makes outcomes very clear. It also gives the staff a way to assess or reflect on the accomplishments of the meeting. Using specific objectives builds pride... agenda lists invite "ho hums" and convey "nothing much will happen."

After the content component, the *what,* you need to think about the *how.* How will the meeting be structured? Large group, small groups? What process for participation will be used? If your faculty has had Tribes training, they will welcome meeting in a community circle and small groups. Do not have them divide into on-going grade level or task groups (tribes) at the first meeting, but provide at least one opportunity to meet in pairs, triads or fours. Post the four Tribes agreements in a prominent place, and invite four teachers to review them at the beginning of the meeting. The agreements initiate the new caring culture just as the process and structure do. The language of the agreements can be the same as used in classrooms:

Attentive listening
Appreciation/no put-downs
Right-to-pass/Participate
Mutual respect

They can also be modified for adult meetings (parent groups, school board, staff, community and district meetings) to something like:

Listening with our hearts and heads
Hearing *appreciation*
Choosing to *participate* or observe
Enjoying *mutual respect*

It may be a fine initial task for the faculty to decide which set to use for adults within the school community system. Just be sure to post and keep using one version or another.

Making a plan for the faculty meeting is important, especially as a way to involve others in leadership for the meeting. It is far better to refer to "our plan" than "my plan." The next page contains the form, *A Tribes TLC® Meeting*. It is a modification of the *Learning Experience Form* that Tribes TLC® teachers use to design quality lessons. Some of the terminology has been changed, but the five process components for you to consider are the same.

DESIGNING THE MEETING PLAN

No matter what the length of a meeting, it needs to begin with inclusion, inviting each person to present something about self, expectations, feelings, skills or interests. The question needs to be tailored as closely as possible to the interests of the persons present and a topic of the meeting. Following are some good and not so good examples:

First Tribes faculty meeting after training

Not good *Share the name of a book you have read lately.*

Good *What expectations do you have about using the process of Tribes in our school? (or in staff meetings?)*

Listening with our hearts and heads

◇

Hearing appreciation

◇

Choosing to participate or observe

◇

Enjoying mutual respect

Group or Organization:

A TRIBES TLC® MEETING

1. Provide for *inclusion*—a question, activity, or energizer.

2. Identify the *objective(s)* to be accomplished and the *collaborative/social skills* to be practiced.

Meeting Objective(s): (write)

Collaborative Skills (check)

- ☐ Participating fully
- ☐ Listening attentively
- ☐ Expressing appreciation
- ☐ Reflecting on experience
- ☐ Valuing diversity of culture/ideas
- ☐ Thinking constructively
- ☐ Making responsible decisions
- ☐ Resolving conflict
- ☐ Solving problems creatively
- ☐ Working together on tasks
- ☐ Assessing improvement
- ☐ Celebrating achievement

Social Skills

- ☐ Sharing
- ☐ Listening
- ☐ Respecting
- ☐ No Put Downs
- ☐ Empathizing

Other:

3. Identify the *strategy(ies)*

4. Ask *reflection questions* about what was accomplished

5. Provide an opportunity for *appreciation*

Faculty meeting adopting new reading curricula

Not good *What do you plan to do for Thanksgiving?*

Good *What are your feelings about the new reading curricula?*

Parent meeting

Not good *Which discipline policies need to be changed?*

Good *What skills do you have to promote parent participation in our school? What are your hopes for your student this year?*

The second section of the form, *A Tribes TLC® Meeting,* is where the objectives are stated. Also check off the collaborative or social skills that are being highlighted in the meeting. These skills, as well as the objectives, should be shared with participants.

Example *We have two objectives tonight. We're going to involve everyone in reviewing the basic approach of the new reading program, and while doing so, we'll practice listening attentively to people who are speaking. At the end of the meeting we'll reflect on what we learned and how well we listened to each other.*

Select strategies carefully to enhance participation and to achieve the objectives. Well chosen strategies in small and large groups give people the opportunity to work together.

Last but hardly least, jot down *reflection questions* that you or your co-facilitators will ask at the end of the meeting. This is the evaluation of how well the objectives were met. Phrase the questions close to the language of the objectives. Based on the example objectives cited above for the parent meeting, a quick assessment could be made by a large audience. Example:

Question 1 *How many people can leave tonight and tell someone else what the basic approach of the new reading program is?* (Ask for a show of hands.)

Question 2 *If you were to rate how well people listened to each other, would you give us a grade of A, B or C?* (Ask for a raise of hands after calling out each grade.)

Always lead applause after assessments with large groups.

Reflection questions also can be written, shared in small groups, collected, summarized and then reported to participants at a future meeting.

Finally, never forget to provide an opportunity for people to thank and appreciate each other. As brief as they may be, appreciation statements are key to building the caring community culture. They may also mean more to someone at the meeting than has anything else.

Keeping the meeting plans in a notebook is especially important as you and others facilitate many meetings with the school. After awhile the five step plan will be internalized so well in your head that using the process will be almost automatic. Inclusion, listening, helping people feel valued, and being a leader who involves everyone in planning and community problem-solving will become your respected style and reputation.

It's that Tom Sawyer method again . . . getting everyone to work together!

THE NEW LEADER FOR THE NEW SCHOOL SYSTEM

Phillip Schlechty in his fine new book, *Inventing Better Schools,* cites changes that must be made in schools so that all activity focuses on students and their needs.[4] We believe his suggestions are congruent with what the process of Tribes can bring about. Schlechty envisions that the role of the principal and the superintendent will change. *Both will function as "leaders of leaders." They will manage by results rather than by programs and inspire others to manage by results as well. Values and vision, rather than programs and rules, will drive the system...School administrators will identify problems to be solved, and engage others to solve them.*

CHAPTER 6

Sustaining and Extending the Culture

Your faculty has been trained in the Basic twenty-four hour Tribes TLC® course and you have begun to use the caring process of Tribes in faculty meetings. People are still floating in the experience of the training, and perhaps sharing how students are responding to being in community circles and using the agreements. One day a question begins to haunt you: "How can we sustain the process of Tribes over a long period of time?" Facing this question is every bit as important as planning the initial training for your faculty. Much has been learned throughout the years from schools and districts that have succeeded in managing long-term implementation and embedding the caring Tribes culture into their systems.

This chapter highlights some steps that have proven to be most effective.

This is a developmental process and not all there at once.

SUSTAINING THE CULTURE	EXTENDING THE CULTURE
Live the Tribes TLC® process	Train district trainers
Structure staff learning groups (tribes)	Extend to parent and community groups
Involve teachers in reflective practice	Transfer responsibility for management
Schedule regular connection time	Celebrate
Assess progress	

LIVE THE TRIBES TLC® PROCESS

A two-year study made by the National Foundation for the Improvement in Education on high-functioning schools concluded that quality professional development is not a program or an activity, but an ethos . . . a way of being which is suffused throughout teachers' working lives in the context of the school.[1] This describes how the caring culture (ethos) of Tribes becomes the relational environment, value system and normative behavior among teachers and school leaders in a school. Every interaction can be a moment of practice and modeling. Using the Tribes agreements, living inclusion, listening with heart as well as head and expressing appreciation reinforces the new way of learning and being together. The more that you and your teachers use the process, not only with students but with each other, the more it will "stick and spread." The culture of caring is contagious. It's really a bit like chocolate. The more you eat the more you want.

STRUCTURE LEARNING GROUPS

We are convinced as are many educators that "restructuring schools" should be about restoring connections, creating a caring climate and community rather than switching roles, tinkering with policy, inviting in more experts or shuffling curriculum.[2] Structuring supportive groups (tribes) throughout the system formalizes connections and re-cultures the school into a working community of trust and

respect. Once connected to others within small groups, everyone gains a sense of belonging (inclusion), a sense of value (influence) and social support (community).

The most successful Tribes TLC® schools have structured on-going faculty tribes for collegial support, collaborative planning, problem-solving, reflective practice and assessment. Innumerable studies indicate that on-going professional development fosters collegiality for the teaching staff and gains for students.

Faculties use grade-level groups, cross grade level groups and mixed groups composed of certified and classified staff. Some schools have both grade level and mixed groupings. One Principal shared her delight in being a member of a mixed group, composed of a second grade teacher, an eighth grade teacher, a bus driver and a school secretary. She wrote, "Never before have I felt so connected to people in our school, nor have I learned so much about our students."

Roland Barth, Director of the Principal's Center at Harvard University, is convinced that:

> The most powerful form of learning, the most sophisticated form of staff development comes not from listening to the good words of others, but from sharing what we know with others. Learning comes more from giving than receiving. By reflecting on what we do, by giving it a coherence, and sharing and articulating our craft knowledge, we make meaning, we learn.[3]

In addition to planning, problem-solving and communicating information, the primary purpose of regular faculty tribe meetings is to discuss classroom implementation of the Tribes TLC® process. Issues typically considered may be:

- What's working—what's not working?
- Teaching the agreements to Kindergarten kids
- Facilitating the community circle
- Integrating curricula into Tribes strategies

- Transferring responsibility to tribes
- Making group problem-solving work well
- Moving groups into research and inquiry projects
- Practicing mutual respect.

Throughout all of the meetings the caring process of Tribes is practiced, using the agreements, providing inclusion, working through issues of influence, reflecting and giving appreciation. Leadership is shared between the principal and faculty leaders.

Typically, a team of two or three teachers plan the meetings with the principal and then facilitate the meeting. Those emerging as willing facilitators are the guides who can advocate and help to sustain the process within the faculty.

USE PEER COACHING GROUPS

Many faculties use peer coaching or learning buddies to help teachers reflect on their use of Tribes. This involves pairs within each tribe becoming on-going partners, inviting each other to brief (10–15 minute) observations of teaching with the process. The partners need to have reached a level of trust within their tribes, with each other, and commit to mutually respecting each others diverse skills and style. Both need to agree that the observations will enable them to learn and grow.

To prepare for the exchange, each partner needs to specify what he or she would like the other partner

Harry, the principal

to observe. The teacher being observed should jot down her own self-reflections before the partners debrief. While observing, the partners follow the practice of the Tribes Pelican "Reflection" who simply asks, "What's happening now?" Specific actions and communication between the teacher and students are noted without comment or judgment. Observers look for the great moments as well as the glitches that may occur. In the debriefing, the partner who was observed shares first, commenting on her self-reflections. The partners discuss and record the improvements that each plans to work on, and decide when to do the exchange again. They also may want to share what they learned with the rest of their teacher tribe. Many hearts and heads can be better than one or even two.

SCHEDULE REGULAR CONNECTION TIME

Admittedly, time cannot be created—but it can be allocated differently. Scheduling students to go to recess, lunch or specialists at the same time allows teachers of the same grade level opportunities to meet. The more that teaching is viewed as an eight hour a day profession (with equitable pay), the more that professional development time will become a practice. Throughout the years we have observed that unless Tribes schools established regular blocks of time for teacher groups (tribes) to meet, the school was less than successful in establishing and sustaining the positive culture.

The majority of Tribes TLC® schools build substantial time into their calendars.

- Weekly 2 hour time blocks
- Once a month in-service days
- Quarterly retreat days
- After school to early evening potlucks or pizza
- 7 a.m. coffee and sweets

Many teacher tribes take it upon themselves to meet daily.

> Let's take a half hour walk before leaving today.
>
> Meet in the faculty lounge—15 minutes today.
>
> How about Saturday morning at my house?

Eight teachers from mixed grade level tribes actually met for two years, as a "teacher researcher group." When asked why they took their own time to meet one member said,

> We do not need new information. We need to think about the information we have. We need, in other words, to consider and interpret what we are teaching; we need constantly to ask what we are doing, to the end that our teaching practices are informed by theory.

Another member replied,

> This has been a powerful group that indeed has the energy to change the world in dramatic and meaningful ways…of course it may take the rest of our lives![4]

ASSESS PROGRESS

Assessing and evaluating Tribes TLC® is the best way to "stick and spread" the use of the process within your school or district. A variety of instruments and evaluation designs are being used by Tribes schools throughout the United States, Canada, Australia, and other countries to assess classroom implementation and outcomes. Inasmuch as the impact on student achievement and behavior depends upon adequate training and implementation of the process, the best assessments use two phases over a period of time.

The CenterSource Systems Assessment Kit which was designed and piloted by the Northwest Regional Educational Laboratory, primarily collects information to show schools the extent of use of the components of the Tribes process within classrooms of the school. Research studies on group learning, collaboration and school climate indicate that the greater extent of the use of the components (i.e.: inclusion, active participation, attentive listening, collaboration, reflection, appreciation, etc.), the greater impact will be realized in student learning and behavioral outcomes.

The CenterSource Assessment Kit is user-friendly so that:

- The teachers and administration of a school can have feedback on the progress of use within classroom
- Areas for improvement can be analyzed and made, and

- Long term outcomes can be documented—even without outside evaluators.

A two-year process study in five elementary schools in the *Central Oahu District of Hawaii* shows significant improvement in respect for the diversity of racial and cultural populations.

A three-phase evaluation was designed and used in the *School District of Beloit, Wisconsin.* The first phase focused upon Tribes training sessions and classroom implementation of the process. The second phase collected data indicating the impact of Tribes on student achievement and behavior. A sample among third grade students the second year resulted in this conclusion:

> Thorough and consistent classroom implementation of the Tribes process and higher CTBS-5 reading scores were significantly associated with higher performance on the WRCT for the sample of students. The socio-economic status, minority status and gender status of students were not significantly associated with WRCT performance.

As striking as any assessments or evaluations may be, outcomes such as the following cited by Beloit teachers also can be considered significant:

> I am seeing improved listening skills, classroom ownership/behavior ownership, connections.
>
> Parents have commented positively.

Tribes has become a strategic goal for our school and also one of my own personal goals.

Tribes is a blessing!

TRAIN DISTRICT TRAINERS

An important step in sustaining and extending the Tribes Learning Community culture within your school or district is to have at least two teachers trained as Certified Tribes TLC® trainers. Then they can:

- Train new teachers coming into your school or district in the Basic Tribes TLC® course
- Provide on-going advanced training for teachers previously trained and using Tribes
- Design meetings for parent, community and district groups
- Make presentations
- Train parents, aides, substitutes, and classified staff.

In short, they will be *guides* helping to re-culture the system and build the whole school learning community.

Best of all once a district has Certified Tribes TLC® trainers, training contracts with CenterSource Systems are no longer necessary. It's a bit crazy to listen to a staff person of CenterSource say to someone in a far off town, *"Oh no, you don't need to contract with us for any more training! Let us train two of your best teachers as Certified Tribes Trainers... You'll save a lot of money that way . . . and keep Tribes happening."*

We call this approach *a capacity building model for professional development.* It is much more effective than continually bringing outside trainers into a district. CenterSource will continue to provide new materials to trainers and professional development for the nationwide Certified Tribes TLC® Trainer network. Attending the Tribes Trainer Summer Institute is the best way to have Certified District Trainers upgrade their professional skills. The appendix in the back of this book contains a description of some of the courses now available to Certified Tribes TLC® District trainers. Also contained in the appendix is a fact sheet on the extent of Tribes training and the demographics among the current trainers throughout this and other countries.

EXTEND THE CULTURE TO PARENTS AND COMMUNITY

"But, how can we possibly get more parents involved?" The question haunts just about every school faculty meeting. Nine times out of ten, the conclusion is that *"we've tried but just the few come."* Typically, when parents come to a school meeting they experience this:

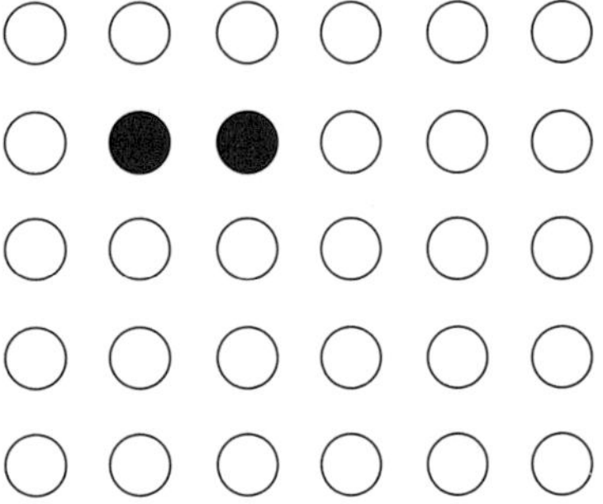

Joe and Thelma are sitting in the second to last row listening to the speaker for the PTA. It is doubtful whether they will ask a question or talk to any other parents. As all of you Tribes experts know, the structure is not designed to give them inclusion; the process is speaker-centered (top-down) and gaining a sense of community is not possible. The caring culture that we hope to extend to parents simply will not happen. Using all that we know about the process of Tribes, parent meetings need to look like this:

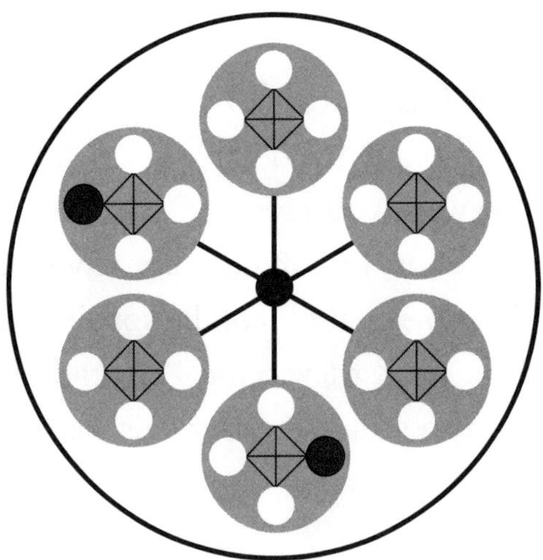

Provide inclusion, inclusion, inclusion! Parents need inclusion too! They long to be able to present who they are, talk about their hopes and dreams for their child, and be acknowledged and appreciated. Restructuring meetings with the process of Tribes not only extends the caring culture into homes, but increases parent involvement. One way or another build on-going parent tribes (support groups) facilitated by trained parents or have those who lead meetings work in partnerships with teachers. No longer is it news that *"when parents are involved at school, their children go farther in school and they go to better schools."*[5]

Initially, a team of Tribes teachers or Certified District Trainers, using the Tribes TLC® Meeting Plan contained in Chapter 5 of this book, can design parent meetings. Page 399 of the Tribes book contains an example of a classroom meeting plan, *Initiating Classroom Parent Tribes.* Throughout all of the meetings the importance of the Tribes agreements needs to be emphasized and practiced. Help parents understand how critical the agreements are in improving the classroom learning environment, and urge that they be used at home.

The system is based on parents reaching parents rather than teachers reaching parents.[6]

—Jeanne Gibbs

Please note Refrigerator magnets with the agreements printed either in English or Spanish can be ordered from CenterSource.

STUDENTS
who maintain long-term membership in classroom tribes will

- Actively participate in the learning process
- Communicate and work well with others
- Value diverse abilities and cultural differences
- Assume responsibility for their own behavior
- Develop critical thinking and collaborative skills
- Improve their sense of self-worth and mastery of academics

A Tribes school is a learning community
where teachers, administrators, students, and parents all enjoy the mutual respect and caring essential for growth and learning

PARENTS
who become involved in the school community will report

- Their children like school better than before
- Positive behavior carries over into the home
- Strengthening protective factors to foster children's resiliency
- Appreciation of their involvement with other parents and the staff of the school
- A new recognition of their own role in their children's education

REACHING ALL BY CREATING TRIBES LEARNING COMMUNITIES

TEACHERS
who are long-term members of faculty planning groups and fully implement the Tribes process in their classroom will

- Spend less time managing student behavior
- Have more time for creative teaching
- Notice that students are retaining what they learn
- Enjoy professional dialogue and supportive colleagues
- Reduce their own levels of stress
- Enjoy teaching more than they have before

ADMINISTRATORS
who use the Tribes process to organize and support their students, staff, and parent community will

- Have fewer student behavior problems
- Benefit from significant and supportive parent involvement
- Over time, improve academic achievement
- Achieve recognition for transforming the school to excellence

The more that the caring culture of Tribes is lived in all of the systems of a school, the more significant will be the outcomes. This next page, which can be found in Chapter One of that big Tribes book, may help everyone in the school community envision the important outcomes that can happen when the Tribes process is used throughout the key systems of the school community. We also suggest that you take time out to re-read, *Building A Parent Network,* in the Tribes book, pages 189–190.

TRANSFER RESPONSIBILITY FOR MANAGEMENT

The organization of Tribes Learning Community peer groups within the systems of the school (faculty, support staff, parents and resource specialists) gives a school leader a flexible structure for decentralizing responsibility. Moreover, everyone uses the same positive agreements and caring process of the new culture. Meetings go better with Tribes! Collaboration becomes a reality whether within a School Site Council, the PTA, or District School Board. One district in the State of Washington even used the Tribes agreements to successfully negotiate with an employee labor union. An Assistant Superintendent of a State Department of Education has made his life easier by having all 70 of the employees in his Personnel Department in tribe groups using the process. They all report that communication, problem-solving and decision making is immensely improved. One woman said, *"I've been working here ten years, and finally feel I'm being heard and appreciated. I love my tribe."*

The basic theory of Tribes is that *unless a person feels included, he or she will act out or drop out.* This certainly also holds true for adults. When a faculty member drops out of participation by being silent at meetings or not coming at all, a valuable resource is lost. Angry interruptions signal a lack of inclusion just as in a student classroom. All long for inclusion and to be sufficiently valued, respected and counted on to assume responsibility.

The role of a wise school leader is to identify problems to be solved, not to solve them. The challenge is to engage the appropriate tribe or tribes to define possible solutions. Then, the celebration is the collaborative action that generates energy throughout the school community.

THE TRIBES SCHOOL

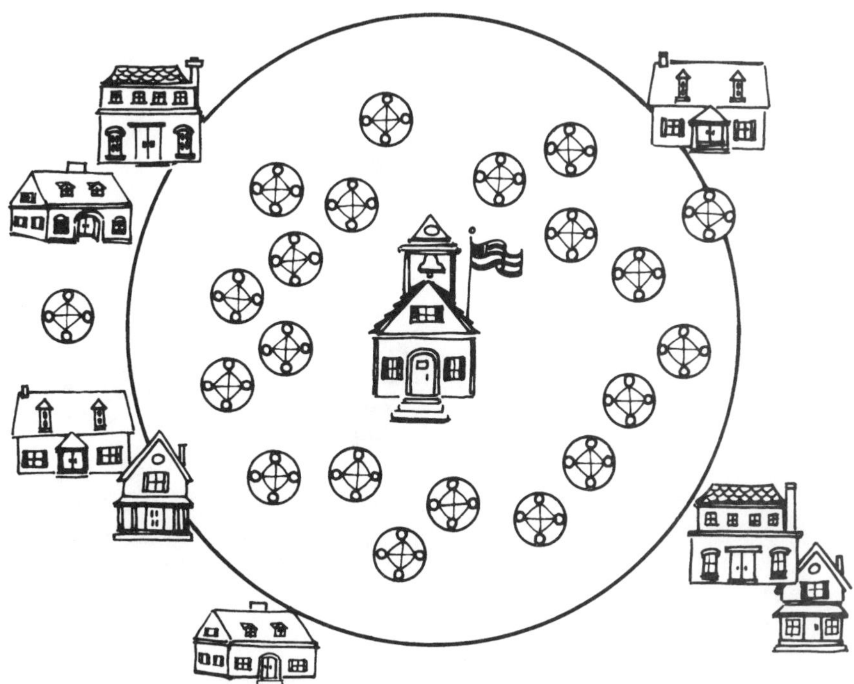

- is student-centered
- actively involves the staff in participative management
- welcomes parents and community involvement in the same process of learning
- everyone has a tribe of their own—students, staff, even parents and community
- at home, families learn to use the same communication skills to strengthen family bonds

Where students, staff and families work together to create a learning environment for healthy human development

Shed light to show the way.
Suggest the choices and let
them feel a personal initiative, and say,
"We did it ourselves!"[7]

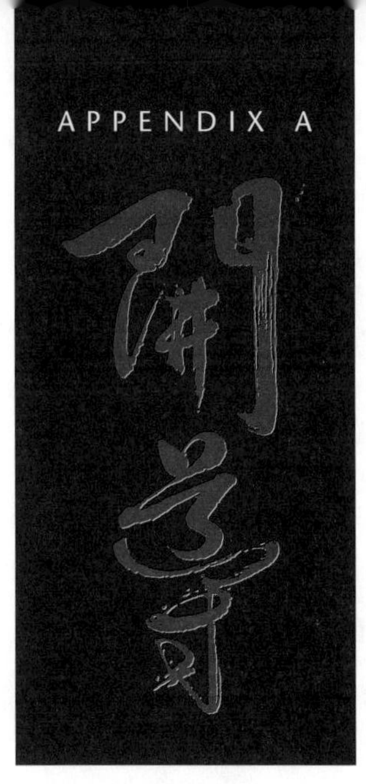

APPENDIX A

Professional Development for Teachers Leads the Way

> There is an emerging consensus across the nation that high-quality professional development is essential to successful education reform. Professional development is the bridge between where educators are now and where they will need to be to meet the new challenges of guiding all students in achieving higher standards of learning.
>
> —Peter Senge

Given that we want to bring about systemic change, the first step is to have the teachers within your school trained in the *Tribes Learning Community*® process. During the training they become members of small "learning communities" . . . grade level planning groups that can continue to support each other in integrating academics into the Tribes process. Training teachers to facilitate the process of Tribes is the most effective way to improve academic learning, lessen behavioral problems, and revitalize a school.

PROFESSIONAL DEVELOPMENT RESOURCES

Given that people working collaboratively toward common goals are the key to school reform and student learning, CenterSource Systems has defined a capacity building model of professional development. "Capacity building" means transferring the professional knowledge, skills and materials to teachers and administrators so that they can conduct on-going training in their own schools rather than depend upon professional trainers over a long period of time.

The steps for a school or district to follow are:

1. **Train all teachers in two Tribes courses—**

YEAR ONE	Either 24-hour Tribes TLC® Basic course Or 24-hour Discovering Gifts in Middle School course
YEAR TWO	24-hour Tribes TLC® Artistry for Learning course for all grade levels

THREE METHODS ARE USED WITHIN DISTRICTS TO INITIATE TEACHER TRAINING—

- Sponsor open trainings for 20–32 Pre-K through 12th grade teachers
- Conduct trainings for all teachers at the different schools

- Identify teams of teachers (6–8 people) and their respective school principals from elementary, middle, or high schools to participate in training, and form a core group within their schools.

2. **After one year, identify and select a qualified group of teachers (at least two per district) to be trained as District Trainers by CenterSource Systems.** As District Trainers, they are provided with quality training materials for all courses designed by CenterSource Systems.

Implementation of the Tribes process and instructional approach is best supported when the school or district arranges sufficient time for the participating teachers to meet together weekly for peer coaching, planning, and integration of curricula into the process.

DESCRIPTIONS OF TRIBES TLC® PROFESSIONAL DEVELOPMENT COURSES

Tribes TLC® Basic Course (24 hours)

The purpose of this 24-hour experiential training is to prepare teachers, administrators and support staff personnel to develop a caring school and classroom environment, and to reach and teach students through an active learning approach that promotes student development, motivation and academic achievement. Participants learn how to:

- Develop a positive learning environment in the classroom and school
- Teach students specific collaborative skills to work well together
- Transfer responsibility to students to help each other learn academic material, and to maintain the positive Tribes agreements and environment
- Use the process for problem-solving and conflict resolution
- Design cooperative learning lesson plans
- Initiate faculty groups for planning, co-coaching and support.

The training time for the basic course may be scheduled over a period of time. However, for the maximum success of the training, the time should be divided into 4 six hour training days—the first two days consecutive. It is particularly important to have the first 12 hours of the training done together.

Tribes TLC® Discovering Gifts in Middle School Course (24 hours)

The purpose of this 24-hour experiential training is to provide a research-based approach for middle level educators to focus on the critical developmental learning needs of young adolescents. The training illuminates how to transform the cultures of middle schools into caring learning communities that support the full range of student growth and development as well as establish academic excellence.

Tribes TLC® Artistry for Learning: The Research-Based Components of the Developmental Process of Tribes Learning Communities® (24 hours)

The purpose of this 24-hour experiential training is to increase the capacity of teachers and administrators within Tribes Learning Community Schools to intensify quality implementation of the research-based process of *Tribes*—thereby to assure that all students, no matter their diversity and ability, achieve higher social, emotional and academic learning. Participants must have completed the 24-hour Basic or Middle School course!

Collaboration: The Art Form of Leadership—Leading for Results in a Tribes Learning Community (12-hours)

School leaders and leadership teams will complete authentic leadership tasks and gain a new exciting view of their roles in reculturing the school. The Tribes collegial team learning experiences will create a professional learning community environment that will support and sustain increasing student learning and achievement. Participants must have completed the 24-hour Basic or Middle School course!

Tribes TLC® After-School Program / Youth Development Course (12 hours)

The purpose of this 12-hour experiential training is to prepare after school educators and youth workers to develop a caring learning center environment and to reach and teach children and youth through an active learning approach that promotes human development, resiliency, and social-emotional competence. Using multiple intelligences, brain compatible learning and cooperative methods, the after-school or community learning center environment will begin to reflect the message of life-long learning, personal development, and social responsibility as the keys to success in the 21st Century.

We highly recommend that

1. Whole faculties are trained together and that the administration demonstrate a total commitment to the training by attending and participating
2. A commitment is made by the faculty to complete both courses over a two-year period of time
3. The faculty has time to meet weekly in grade level co-coaching/planning groups.

On-site Coaching, Classroom Demonstrations, Presentations and Assessment

These support services are very helpful in implementing school or district change through the Tribes process. Dialogue meetings or phone conversations with other Tribes TLC® school administrators and teachers can be arranged by contacting CenterSource Systems.

For additional information contact

CenterSource Systems, LLC
7975 Cameron Drive, Suite 500
Windsor, CA 95492
Ph: 707-838-1061
Fax: 707-838-1062
Email: tribes@tribes.com
Internet: www.tribes.com
1-800-810-1701

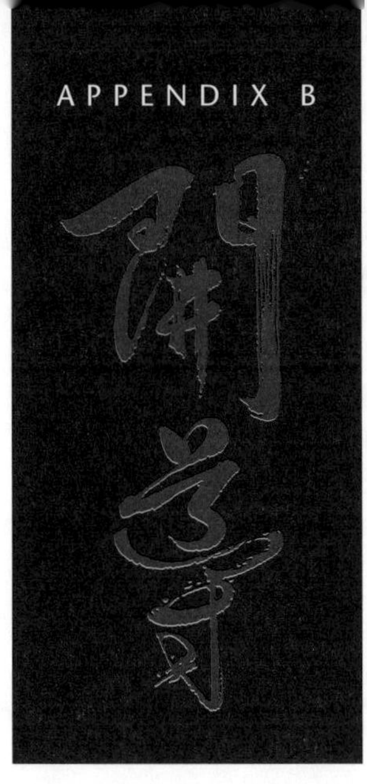

A FACT SHEET ON TRIBES TLC®

THERE ARE CERTIFIED TRIBES TLC® TRAINERS SERVING

All U.S. States and Canada, as well as distant lands such as Australia, New Zealand, Guam, American Samoa, the People's Republic of China, the Dominican Republic, Ecuador, the Northern Marianas, Micronesia, the Marshall Islands, and parts of Africa.

Demographics of Trainers

Certified Tribes TLC® Trainers include individuals of almost all races and ethnic groups. Over one fourth of the 1,300 trainers are bilingual or multilingual. Approximately one third are administrators (Assistant Superintendents, Principals, Coordinators, State Department Officials and Program Managers). There are also Psychologists, Private Consultants, Deacons, University

Instructors and, of course, public and private school classroom teachers, including National Board Certified teachers. The Certified Tribes Trainers have degrees ranging from Bachelors to PhD's. Ages of the trainers range from age 22 to 76. There are trainers living in 42 U.S. states, as well as many other countries.

The Tribes process can be found in

- Public Schools
- Private Schools
- Parochial Schools
- Native American, First Nation, Aboriginal Schools and schools serving other Indigenous populations
- International Schools
- University Programs
- State Departments of Education
- After School Programs
- Recreation Programs
- Family Resource Centers
- Church Groups
- Drug and Alcohol Treatment Centers
- Regional Educational Centers

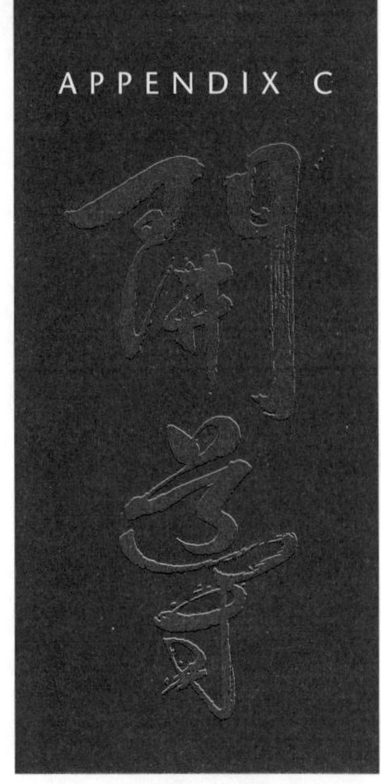

Tribes Learning Communities®— A Model and Promising Program

CASEL

SELect Program

www.casel.org

Tribes TLC® was chosen by the Collaborative for Academic, Social and Emotional Learning (CASEL) as one of 22 SELect Programs by demonstrating the following essential requirements:

- provides outstanding coverage in five essential SEL areas
- has well-designed evaluation demonstrating effectiveness
- offers high-quality professional development.

OJJDP

Promising Program

www.dsgonline.com

Tribes TLC® is included in the Office of Juvenile Justice Delinquency Prevention's

Model Programs Guide, which was developed to assist educational practitioners and communities in "implementing evidence-based prevention and intervention programs that can make a difference in the lives of children and communities." The Guide's ratings are derived from four dimensions of program effectiveness:

- conceptual framework of the program
- program fidelity
- evaluation design
- empirical evidence demonstrating the prevention or reduction of problem behaviors, the reduction of risk factors, and the enhancement of protective factors.

CSAP's Western CAPT Promising Program

http://captus.samhsa.gov/western/western.cfm
The Western Center for the Application of Prevention Technologies (funded by the Center for Substance Abuse Prevention) has identified Tribes Learning Communities® as "an evidence-based promising practice that [has] quantitative data showing positive outcomes in delaying substance abuse over a period of time." CSAP prevention strategies focus on both risk and protective factors in the areas of family, school, individual, peer, society and/or community.

Helping America's Youth
Level 3 Program

www.helpingamericasyouth.gov

Tribes Learning Communities® is recognized in the evidence-based *Community Guide to Helping America's Youth* (HAY). The Guide represents a collaborative effort of nine federal departments, including the U.S. Department of Education, Department of Justice, Department of Health and Human Services, Department of Housing and Urban Development, Office of National Drug Control Policy, and National and Community Service. Tribes is recognized as a program that displays "a strong theoretical base and has been demonstrated to prevent delinquency and other child and youthful problems or reduce risk factors and enhance protective factors for them."

Visit www.tribes.com or contact CenterSource for additional information and supporting documentation.

APPENDIX D

EVALUATION OF TRIBES LEARNING COMMUNITIES

Evaluation of Tribes Learning Community Schools has shown that:

- Tribes TLC has a positive impact on classroom environment
- teachers spend less time managing student behavior
- students are less likely to be referred for disciplinary problems
- the Tribes process helps teachers address academic standards
- students in well-implemented classrooms score significantly higher on standardized tests than students from comparison groups
- teachers report increased staff collegiality and planning.

WestEd conducted a 2-year evaluation of Tribes TLC that involved administering surveys in 13 schools and collecting standardized test results for 40 Tribes schools and 80 control schools. The evaluators found that:

- the Tribes TLC process was fully implemented
- Tribes was seen as a vehicle for facilitating continuous school improvement
- there was evidence of improved student inclusion, collaboration, respect for multicultural populations, sense of value, resiliency, and student engagement
- students and staff enjoyed safe and supportive classroom and school environments
- teachers and principals reported declines in student referrals and suspensions
- there was evidence of better classroom management and increased teacher collaboration and planning
- three-quarters of teachers reported that the Tribes process helped them to address academic standards and helped students master standards
- 2nd and 5th grade reading and math scores increased more in high-growth Tribes schools than in comparison schools.

The **School District of Beloit** in Wisconsin conducted a 3-year evaluation of the Tribes process that included more than 3,000 elementary and middle school students. Dr. Derick Kiger presented the study at the 2001 American Education Research Association Annual Meeting and earned the First Place Instructional Program Evaluation Award.

Evaluators found that:

- 4th graders from Tribes classrooms where the program was well-implemented scored significantly higher on the CTBS than students from less well-implemented Tribes classrooms

- sixty percent of the teachers reported that they spent less time managing student behavior because of the Tribes process.

In **Tulsa, Oklahoma**, Dr. Judith Holt used a randomized design to conduct an evaluation of the impact of Tribes on discipline referrals at a middle school. The study found that:

- students based in Tribes classrooms were significantly less likely (27%) than non-Tribes students (73%) to be referred to the principal's or counselor's office for disciplinary problems of all types, including disruptive behavior, refusal to work or follow directions, and fighting.

The **Central Oahu School District** in the State of Hawaii conducted a study of 17 elementary schools that implemented the process of Tribes. The evaluators found that:

- mutual respect was the most common practice for students and faculty.

Fifty-five classroom teachers and their students in **Spring Branch ISD** in Texas participated in a Tribes evaluation survey, which found that in Tribes classrooms:

- teachers spent less time managing student behavior
- teachers had more time for creative teaching
- students saw new learning as "fun"
- mutual respect was evidenced through behaviors
- group behaviors changed even at bus stops as students began accepting more responsibility for their behavior.

APPENDIX E

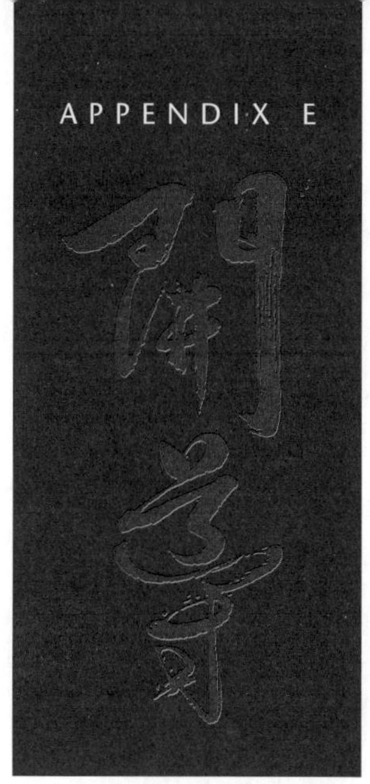

What Is It About Tribes?

The Research-Based Components of the Developmental Process of Tribes Learning Communities®

Bonnie Benard

This important new book, researched and written by Bonnie Benard, is an in-depth response to questions that more and more people, concerned today about improving the quality of education, have been asking. In one way or another many have been inquiring, "What is it about the *process* of "Tribes" that makes it work so well in so many schools, cultures and countries? What is it that helps all kinds of kids love learning and achieve? What is it that makes teaching easier and more enjoyable for teachers?" We knew that there was only one person who could help us to respond by documenting the efficacy of the approach underlying the process known simply as "Tribes" or formally as Tribes Learning Communities.® Of course, we called upon Bonnie Benard of West Ed, who with her amazing contextual skills brought hundreds of research studies and literature references into enlightening coherence. It is our hope that readers will discover why and how implementing the core components of the process of Tribes transforms people, classrooms and schools—not because the approach is a curriculum to be taught or a program to be replicated—but because it is an on-going student-centered active-learning process that everyone in a school lives daily and owns. This book also will prove to be invaluable in the writing of grants, accessing other resources, designing parent, community and district programs. More than all, we hope as you deepen your understanding of the transformational process, you will use it in endless ways to enhance belonging, student motivation, competence and meaningful learning. Keep in mind the advice that experienced Tribes teachers often tell new teachers... "Trust the Process—It works!" —Jeanne Gibbs

---

Bonnie Benard is a nationally- and internationally-known figure in the field of prevention and youth development theory, policy, and practice and is credited with introducing resiliency theory and applications to the fields of education and prevention. She holds a Master's Degree in Social Work and is currently a Senior Program Associate with the Health & Human Development Program at WestEd's Oakland, California office. In this capacity, she has led the development of a statewide resilience and youth development assessment for the California Department of Education of the protective factors in students' families, schools, communities, and peer groups. Her most recent publication, *Resiliency: What We Have Learned* (2004), synthesizes a decade and more of resiliency research and describes what application of the research looks like in our most successful efforts to support young people.

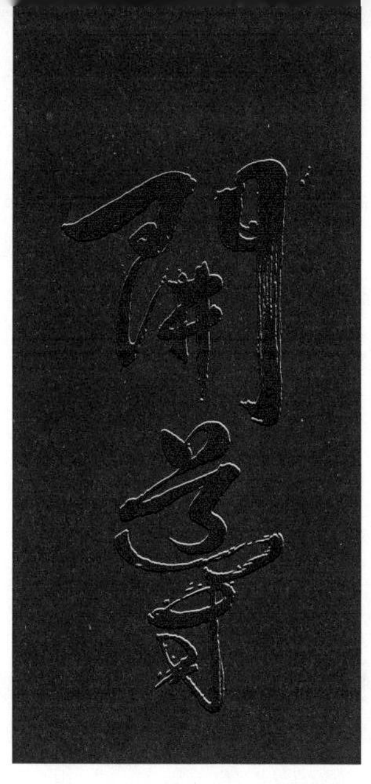

NOTES

CHAPTER ONE

1. Tribes TLC® is the trade and service mark used to designate the quality training and materials of CenterSource Systems, LLC, and to distinguish the proprietary work of Jeanne Gibbs, developer of the Tribes process from any and all other persons claiming to be developers or claiming to be trainers for the concepts within the books, *Tribes, A New Way of Learning and Being Together* (CenterSource Systems, 2001), *Discovering Gifts in Middle School* (CenterSource Systems, 2001), *Reaching All by Creating Tribes Learning Communities* (CenterSource Systems, 2006), *Engaging All by Creating High School Learning Communities* (CenterSource Systems, 2007), and *Guiding Your School Community to Live a Culture of Caring and Learning* (CenterSource Systems, 2007).
2. Huang, Chungliang Al, and Lynch, Jerry, *Mentoring the Tao of Giving and Receiving Wisdom,* San Francisco: Harper Collins, 1994.
3. List developed by the Association of Washington School Principals, 1995.
4. Fullen, Michael, "Coordinating Top-Down and Bottom-Up Strategies for Educational Reform," Elmore, R.F. and Furhrman, S.H.

(Eds.), *The Governance of Curriculum: The 1994 Yearbook of the Association for Supervision and Curriculum Development,* Alexandria, VA, 1994.

5. Conference report: Association of Washington State School Principals, 1995.
6. Maya Angelou delivered the poem *On the Pulse of Morning* ©1993 at the inauguration ceremony of President Clinton, from *The Complete Collected Poems of Maya Angelou,* New York: Random House, 1994, p. 272.
7. Sergiovanni, Thomas, J. *Leadership for the Schoolhouse,* San Francisco: Jossey-Bass, 1996, p. 9–15.
8. Prawatt, R., "The Role of the Principal in Developing Learning Communities," *Wingspan: The Pedamorphosis Communiqué,* 1993, p. 7–9.
9. Senge, Peter, *The Fifth Discipline: The Art and Practice of the Learning Organization,* New York: Doubleday, 1990.
10. Levinson, Jay Conrad, *The Way of the Guerrilla: Achieving Success and Balance as an Entrepreneur in the 21st Century,* New York: Houghton Mifflin, 1997.
11. Barth, Roland, "The Leader as Learner," *Education Week,* March 5, 1997.
12. Grossman, Jack, H., "The Art of Good Teaching," *Sky Magazine,* Delta Airlines, March, 1995, p. 24–28.
13. Miller, Ron, *What Are Schools For? Holistic Culture in American Culture,* Brandon, VT: Holistic Education Press, 1990.

CHAPTER TWO

1. Stolp, Stephen, and Smith, Stuart, "School Culture and Climate: The Role of the Leader," *OSSC Bulletin:* Oregon School Study Council, 1995.
2. Stolp, Stephen, "Leadership for School Change," *ERIC Digest,* June 1994, p. 91.
3. Bruner, Jerome, *The Culture of Education,* Cambridge, MA: Harvard University, 1996.

4. Saphier, J. and D'Auria, J., "How to Bring Vision to School Improvement Through Outcomes, Commitments and Beliefs," Carlisle, MA: Research for Better Teaching, Inc., 1993.

5. Hill, P.T., Foster, G.D., and Gendler, T., *High Schools with Character in Today's Youth,* Santa Monica, CA: Rand, 1990.

6. The mission of Tribes is to assure the healthy development of every child so that each has the knowledge, skills and resiliency to be successful in a rapidly changing world.

   The goal for a Tribes school is to engage all teachers, administrators, students, and families in working together as a learning community that is dedicated to caring and support, active participation and positive expectations for all students.

CHAPTER 3

1. Sergiovanni, Thomas, *Leadership of the Schoolhouse,* San Francisco, Jossey-Bass, 1996, p. 97.

2. Sobel, Thomas, "What Do Superintendents Want?" *Education Week,* May, 1997.

3. Comer, James, "Educating Poor Minority Children," *Scientific American* 259(5), November, 1988, p. 42–48.

4. Meier, Deborah, "Reinventing Teaching," *Teacher's College Record,* 1992-93(4), p. 594–609.

5. Sergiovanni, Thomas, *Leadership of the Schoolhouse,* San Francisco: Jossey-Bass, 1996, p. 102.

6. Likona, Thomas, "Four Strategies for Fostering Character Development in Children," *Phi Delta Kappan,* 1988, Vol. 69, No. 6, p. 421.

7. Rossi, Robert, and Stringfield, Samuel, "What We Must Do For Students Placed At Risk," *Phi Delta Kappan,* 1995 Vol. 77, No. 1, p. 73–76.

8. McKnight, John. "Are Social Service Agencies the Enemy of Community?" *Utne Reader,* July/August, 1992, p. 89–90.

9. Seashore, Lois, Marks, Helen, and Kruse, Sharon, "Teacher's Professional Community in Restructuring

Schools," *American Educational Research Journal,* Winter, 1996, Vol. 33, No. 4, p. 757–798.

10. Hoerr, Thomas, "Making Time for Collegiality," *Education Week,* April 23, 1997.
11. Lewis, Anne C., "A New Consensus Emerges on the Characteristics of Good Professional Development," *The Harvard Education Letter,* Vol. XIII, Number 3, May/June, 1997.
12. Hoerr, Thomas, "Making Time for Collegiality," *Education Week,* April 23, 1997.
13. "Kirkland School Chief Finalist for Superintendent of the Year," The Daily News, Longview, Washington, January 11, 1995, p. 6.
14. Senge, Peter, *The Fifth Discipline, The Art and Practice of the Learning Community,* New York: Doubleday/ Currency, 1991.
15. Klapper, Michael, Berlin, Donna, and White, Arthur, *Professional Development: Starting Point for Systemic Reform,* Cognosos: *The National Center for Science Teaching and Learning Research Quarterly,* Vol. 3, No. 4, Autumn 1994.
16. Gibbs, Jeanne, *Reaching All by Creating Tribes Learning Communities,* Windsor, CA: CenterSource Systems, 2006.

CHAPTER FOUR

1. The remarks made by Aileen Hokama, Superintendent of the Central Oahu District, Honolulu, HI are based on a recorded interview with the author, April 13, 1998.
2. Rogers, Everett, "Diffusion of the Idea Beyond Way," *Break Through—Emerging New Thinking,* New York: Walker and Co. 1988, p. 240–248.
3. Florin, P. and Chavis, D.M., *Community Prevention and Substance Abuse Prevention,* San Jose, CA: Bureau of Drug Abuse Services, County of Santa Clara, May 1990.
4. Ibid: Rogers.

CHAPTER FIVE

1. Gibbs, Jeanne, *Reaching All by Creating Tribes Learning Communities,* Windsor, CA: CenterSource Systems, 2006, p. 8.

2. *SCANS Report for America 2000: What Work Requires of Schools,* Washington D.C.: Secretary's Commission on Achieving Necessary Skills, U.S. Department of Labor, 1991. (See page 20 in *Reaching All by Creating Tribes Learning Communities* for a list of the skills.)

3. The J.C. Penney Foundation distributes $38M per year to schools to create environments for learning.

4. Schlechty, Phillip C., *Inventing Better Schools: An Action Plan for Educational Reform,* San Francisco: Jossey-Bass, 1997, p. 70–71.

CHAPTER 6

1. Renyi, Judith, "Building Learning into the Teaching Job," *Educational Leadership,* February, 1998, p. 70–71.

2. Newmann, Fred M., *School-wide Professional Community Issues in Restructuring Schools,* Center on Organization and Restructuring of Schools, Issue Report No. 6, 1994, p. 1–2.

3. Barth, Roland, *Improving Schools from Within,* San Francisco, CA: Jossey-Bass, 1995.

4. Quotes are from Suzanne James-Peters and Catherine Lutes-Koths of the Tribes Teacher Researcher Group, Solano County, California. Both are Certified Tribes Trainers.

5. "Parent Involvement in Schools: Clarifying Complex Education Issues," *EdSource Report,* September 1994.

6. Gibbs, Jeanne, *Reaching All by Creating Tribes Learning Communities,* Windsor, CA: CenterSource Systems, 2006, p. 190.

7. Huang, Chungliang Al and Lynch, Jerry, *Mentoring: The Tao of Giving and Receiving Wisdom,* San Francisco: Harper Collins, 1995, p. 102.

ABOUT THE AUTHOR

Jeanne Gibbs
Founder and Author
Tribes Learning Communities

Jeanne has spent her professional career studying, writing and implementing systemic processes and programs to support children's development and prevent youth problems. Her perspective on human development is a systems approach that encourages schools, families and communities to create healthy environments in which children can grow and learn. The developmental culture and educational process now known as "Tribes Learning Communities" evolved out of years of studies Jeanne has pursued to synthesize a wealth of literature pertaining to the ecology of human development and learning. She is convinced that well being and success for students is not a result of curriculum, instruction and assessment—nor of intelligence—but the result of a school finally focusing on the growth and whole human development of its students in all aspects of their individual uniqueness and brilliance. The vision takes on reality whenever a school system focuses first on creating and sustaining a caring culture in which children truly are able to discover themselves and succeed.

Jeanne supervised implementations of the community learning process throughout hundreds of schools and youth-serving agencies for more than ten years while managing a non-profit corporation, which she had founded. Though serving as the executive director, she continued to research, refine and author publications—until her first formal retirement. Since then, Jeanne has retired many times—none of which last long due to her to passionate purpose. Ever-growing requests from schools throughout the United States, Canada, Australia and other countries for professional development and quality materials led her to establish CenterSource Systems in 1995 as "the home of Tribes."

Her primary interest now centers on the potential of school reform being achieved through reflective Learning Communities that are responsive to the developmental and learning needs of their students. It is no surprise that people across the country know Jeanne for her warm and generous spirit… and ability to build community wherever she goes.